THE PUSAN PERIMETER, KOREA, 1950

Bibliographies of Battles and Leaders

THE PUSAN PERIMETER, KOREA, 1950

An Annotated Bibliography

Compiled by
Paul M. Edwards

Bibliographies of Battles and Leaders, Number 11
Myron J. Smith, Jr., Series Adviser

Greenwood Press
Westport, Connecticut • London

Library of Congress Cataloging-in-Publication Data

Edwards, Paul M.
   The Pusan perimeter, Korea, 1950 : an annotated bibliography /
compiled by Paul M. Edwards.
      p.   cm.—(Bibliographies of battles and leaders, ISSN
1056-7410 ; no. 11)
   Includes bibliographical references and indexes.
   ISBN 0-313-28740-6
   1. Korean War, 1950-1953—Bibliography.   2. Korean War, 1950-1953—
United States—Bibliography.   3. Korean War, 1950-1953—Campaigns—
Korea (South)—Pusan—Bibliography.   I. Title.   II. Series.
Z3316.E39   1993
[DS919]
016.951904'2—dc20   93-2586

British Library Cataloguing in Publication Data is available.

Library of Congress Catalog Card Number: 93-2586
ISBN: 0-313-28740-6
ISSN: 1056-7410

First published in 1993

Greenwood Press, 88 Post Road West, Westport, CT 06881
An imprint of Greenwood Publishing Group, Inc.

Printed in the United States of America

∞™

The paper used in this book complies with the
Permanent Paper Standard issued by the National
Information Standards Organization (Z39.48-1984).

10 9 8 7 6 5 4 3 2 1

CONTENTS

vi   Contents

SERIES FOREWORD

The Greeks at Thermopylae, the Crusades, the Armada campaign, Trafalgar, Verdun, Gettysburg, El Alamein, Pork Chop Hill, Khe Sahn, the Falklands, and "Desert Storm" are only a few of the many campaigns and battles, large and small, which have been fought down through the ages. Of course, each of these operations had leaders ranging in quality from Leonidas at Thermopylae to the group think of Vietnam and all featured diverse strategy, tactics, and weaponry. It appears to be mankind's unhappy lot that war has been and apparently will for sometime continue to be a growth industry, despite centuries of horror-filled record-keeping and preventative lessons available for the learning. With only a few exceptions, monographic bibliographies of individual battles and leaders (our series title admittedly, is borrowed from the famous American Civil War history), campaigns and weapons have not been compiled previously. Contributors to this series while thus breaking new ground have also constructed works suitable for wide general audiences. These tools may profitably by employed at every level from high school through graduate university and by the casual researcher/buff as well as the dedicated scholar.

Each volume begins with a narrative overview of the topic designed to place its subject within the context of specific wars, societies, and times; this introduction evaluates the significance of the leader, battle, or technology under study. Each work points to key archival and document collections as well as printed primary and secondary sources. Citations are numbered, allowing easy access via the index(es). Individual volumes may present discussion of their citations in styles ranging from bibliographical essays to individually annotated entries and some titles provide chronologies and suitable appendix(es).

It is my hope as editor that these bibliographies of battles and leaders will enable broad audiences to select and work with the best items available within literature and to benefit from the wisdom of some of today's leading military scholars.

Myron J. Smith, Jr., Series Adviser
Tusculum College
Greeneville, Tennessee

PREFACE

When the military forces of the North Korean government crossed the 38th parallel during the night of 25 June 1950 they began a conflict which continues today. South Korean forces, despite years of training and development under the American staffed Korean Military Advisory Group, failed to hold their ground. Within days what some had hoped was a minor probe turned out to be the first stage of a massive war effort which would, before it was over, engage the military machines of more than 30 nations.

When the United States, in conjunction with the United Nations, entered the war it did so in a manner hardly designed for success. Poorly trained, and equipped with the remains of World War II, the first Americans discovered they could not stop the advance. As the days passed the United States became more and more concerned about survival in Korea. Retreat after retreat became necessary as the North Korean armies poured men and weapons into the struggle.

The only real response was to hold ground as long as possible, then to retreat, trading land and lives for time as replacement forces from nearly two dozen nations were being procured. In this process the United States and the troops of the Republic of Korea moved further south and east until there was nothing left but a perimeter formed around the essential port of Pusan.

There, steadily resupplied and reenforced, the United Nations troops took a stand against the increasingly extended North Korean armies, and held. While bulge after bulge was driven into the line the Perimeter held. Finally, in conjunction with MacArthur's landing at Inchon, the battled Eighth Army was to break the siege and began moving north.

Materials dealing with these early days are not as plentiful as one might expect. At the time there was not a lot to say about American unpreparedness, its inability to stop the North Koreans, nor about the fact the United States was so taken by surprise. Retreat makes good news copy but it is not the stuff of which popular and academic inquiries flourish. This was not a successful period and, as it turned out, it was not a successful or popular war. However, there are an increasing number of articles, books, and monographs being produced concerning the war.

Materials Included

Included in this bibliography are materials which deal with this early phase of the conflict, called the Pusan Perimeter. That is, it deals with relevant pre-war information, the invasion, the series of retreats, the forming and defense of the perimeter, and the breakout. Included are official and unofficial reports, documents, surveys, and monographs written, or available, in English.

During the Korean Conflict ground units were required by regulation to keep official records and these records, running from units the size of a battalion to corps and armies, are available. These consist of action reports, war diaries, battle narratives, daily reports and intelligence information. Associated with these are the reports of air naval actions and Air Force, Navy and Marine unit materials. These include reports of the Eighth Army, as well as its primary components (I, IX, X corps and the six combat divisions) which are located in Suitland, Maryland.

Most of these records are kept at the Army's Center of Military History in conjunction with the National Archives. A good deal of the meat of these reports has been published in the six volume "histories" prepared by able military historians, or in the official series The United States Army in Korea.

In the past few years more and more military analysis has taken place concerning the early phases of the Korean Conflict and these can be found in the service institution's libraries or at the Command and Staff College Library at Leavenworth, Kansas.   Other related works are available at the United States Marine Corps History (Division) Museum at the Washington Navy Yard, the Special Collection of the Mitchell memorial Library, the Harry S Truman Presidential Library and the Center for the Study of the Korean Conflict in Independence, Missouri.

Materials Excluded

Other than for occasional reference I have excluded picture books, "table top" works, collections of drawings about weapons or uniforms (except when they relate directly to the Perimeter), newspaper items (available in the New York Public Library), or general histories or items which seem to repeat materials easily found elsewhere.

Period Covered

While it seems necessary to take a look at some of the pre-war events to better understand what happened, this bibliography tries to stick to the phase of the war identified as the Pusan Perimeter; that is, 25 June 1950 to 22 September 1950. Some may find fault with my inclusion of the early invasion period, or the many retreats, counterattacks, and defenses prior to the pullback to Pusan, but my understanding of the events of

this war lead me to believe that these are all totally
interconnected.

ACKNOWLEDGMENTS

The compilation of an extensive bibliography, especially in an area where little previous work has taken place, requires the help and encouragement of a lot of people. Many persons have provided aid and service which they consider to be no more than the daily routine of their assignments, but for which I am most grateful. Others have gone far beyond any expectations of employment or assignment and have taken the merit of the work upon themselves to make a very significant contribution.

I wish to acknowledge the help of the librarians and staff at Mid-Continent Public Library, Jackson County, Missouri; the Kansas City, Missouri Public Library (especially the Three Trails Branch), the Denver, Colorado, the St. Louis, Missouri, the Chicago, Illinois, and New York City Public Library.

Thanks also to the reference and document librarians at the University of Missouri at Kansas City, Washburn University Library in Topeka, Kansas, Dr. Tom Peterman at Park College, Kansas City, Missouri, Dr. Mary Lou Goodyear, Acting Director, the Sterling C. Evans Library at Texas A & M University, the librarians and staff of Baker University, Leawood, Kansas, the librarians at Southwestern Missouri State University in Springfield, Missouri.

Thanks also to the Dr. Zobrist and the highly professional staff of the Truman Presidential Library in Independence, Missouri; to the professional staff of the Linda Hall Library of Kansas City, Missouri; to Dan Holt of the Eisenhower Presidential Library and Archives in Abilene, Kansas, and to Louise A. Arnold-Friend, reference historian at the United States Army Military History Institute, Carlisle Barracks, Pennsylvania, and the staff at the United States Air University Library.

Particular thanks to the much overworked members of the library staff of the Command and Staff Library at the Command and Staff College, Leavenworth, Kansas, who have compiled one of the most complete collections of military sources available.

Special thanks to the Center for the Study of the Korean War located in Independence, Missouri. This special library and archives, centering on personal accounts of the War, is becoming increasingly valuable as a research tool. Of particular help Joni Wilson, the Executive Secretary of the Center, has provided insights, careful consideration, and final readings of the manuscript which has avoided errors of commission and omission. To Joni, and the Center, my appreciation.

I was quick to discover that the Korean War, while still a mystery to most persons, became a topic of interest for those to whom it was introduced. Questions about lost or rare books set off searches beyond wildest imagination and with help I found materials in the deepest basements of public libraries; discovered that one of the best sources of military publications is the library of a local religious college; and located Korean Veterans who upon hearing of our interest, joined the search, and several book lovers who applied their considerable talents to the location of materials.

Of these individuals I owe special appreciation to Roger Revell, Frank Kelley, Jack Garnier, Linda Booth, Carolyn Riddle, Robert Kozuki, Tom Peterman, and Lee Pement.

Thanks as well to Professor Myron J. Smith, Jr. of Tusculum College Library, Greeneville, Tennessee, who took time to work with me on the selection of this topic, and to Mildred Vasan of Greenwood Press who has been a kind and efficient editor.

Paul M. Edwards, Ph.D.
Independence, Missouri

COMMENT ON SOURCES

Since that long summer night in June of 1950 when the Korean War began, the United States has been involved in several significant military activities. For a long time there was very little information available on the Korean Conflict, or War as it became in the late 1950s. Most of what was available came from quick adaptations of "on the spot" experiences and memories, or a few hard written official efforts. Many of the early works were written in 1952 and 1953 as if the war had ended in 1951, and they reflect a strange attitude toward what they seemed to consider the lesser war of late 1952 and early 1953.

A good percentage of the historical efforts made available in the 1960s and 1970s tended to be confined to accounts "borrowed" from the few and very limited official histories that had painstakingly been produced. Often published works simply repeated the generalizations previously identified, with little new research and analysis available.

Only recently have some scholarly and well written general histories appeared. But in the main these general histories are popular ones, once again offering little in-depth understanding. In the near half a century following this war, very few detailed accounts, even fewer scholarly monographs, theses and dissertations have been produced. Detailed studies on the various aspects of the Korean War, especially those essential early months have not reached anything like the level of materials produced about either World War II or Vietnam. It has truly been the "forgotten war" in American History.

But it is not undocumented. The difficulty lies in locating these scattered materials which can be found, to a large extent, in the following locations: The National Archives contains the primary documents on the Korean War, as well as the diplomatic, executive and legislative materials dealing with the war; the Modern Military History Headquarters Branch, and the Legislative and Diplomatic Branch, of the National Archives, both located in Washington DC, as well as the Modern Military History Field Branch at the Washington National Records Center in the Federal Building in Suitland Maryland.

The actual size of the document collections is overwhelming. As was true of World War II, every United States Army ground unit from the Army through the infantry regiment level, as well as artillery and armored battalions, were required by military regulation to keep official records. These records consist of action reports, war diaries, battle narratives as well as daily reports and intelligence information. In some instances, the Eighth Army War Diary for example, air support action records were also kept.

At most levels there are official (staff) historians at work. The compilations of Army staff historians is kept at the Army's Center of Military History in Washington DC. Some of this material is available in an official compendium edited by Russell A. Gugeler, <u>Combat Action in Korea</u>, but most of this is as yet unpublished. The typescript of this manuscript is located at the Army's Center of Military History.

Most of the messages between the Joint Chiefs of Staff and the General Headquarters in Tokyo are published in <u>Foreign Relations of the United States</u>, Vol. VII, 1951, parts 1 and 2. Those not published are in the National Archives, Washington DC, Modern Military Records Branch. The Modern Military Records Branch, National Archives has prepared a "Record of Actions

Taken by the Joint Chiefs of Staff Relative to the United Nations Operations in Korea from 25 June to 11 April 1951", a 107 page analysis.

The Reports of the Eighth Army in Korea, as well as its many components (I, IX, X corps and the six combat divisions) are located at the National Archives depository at the Federal Records Center in Suitland, Maryland.

Oral histories of leading military commanders and advisors are to be found at the United States Marine Corps History (Division) and Museum at the Washington Navy Yard, Washington DC; at the Special Collection Department, Mitchell Memorial Library, Mississippi State University; at the MacArthur Memorial Archives in Norfolk, Virginia; and the Harry S Truman Presidential Library at Independence, Missouri.

Several smaller, and private, organizations have been collecting archival materials dealing with the Korean War. The Center for the Study of the Korean Conflict in Independence, Missouri concentrates on the private papers, orders, oral tapes, maps, etc. of the individual soldier.

Unfortunately the valuable action reports of the 34th Infantry Regiment, the 2nd Infantry Division (composed of the 9th and 38th regiments) and the 5th Regimental Combat Team were lost as a result of combat, or retreat, during the hard days of the war. And while some effort was made to recreate those, they are of limited value.

While smaller unit histories are often produced by official historians, most seem to be written by interested amateurs who are able to provide a lot of information, but generally with little analysis. Those available for units during the Pusan Perimeter are listed under the proper section of the bibliography, but the major ones include the 1st Cavalry Division, the 2nd, 3rd, 7th, 24th and 25th Divisions, and the 89th Tank Battalion which are primarily concerned with the units in Korea, and the 7th Division and the 187th Airborne which are only partially concerned with Korea.

Korea was a much photographed war. But still only a limited number of such photographs have ever appeared in print. Most photographs are to be located at the

Still Picture Division, Main Archives and at the Defense Audiovisual Agencies, Still Photographic Depository Anacostia Naval Station, Washington, D. C.

Maps from the Korean War are preserved at the Cartographic and Architectural Branch, Special Archives Division, National Archives, Alexandria, Virginia.

BRIEF HISTORY
OF THE PUSAN PERIMETER

The Korean War has been labeled America's forgotten war. This is perhaps not so true as to suggest that it has always been America's unreal war. It just never seemed to have happened. Few lives, other than those who were directly involved in the fighting, were disturbed by it at all. There were few, if any, requirements or adjustments demanded by the civilian population. There were no restrictions on travel, no rationing, no gas shortages.

Harry S Truman, unlike later presidents, worked to translate the economics of the war into the American economy so if any change was noted most would have found themselves better off because of it.

It was not a real war; that is, not a war for survival. There was little about this conflict in an unknown land to stir the American public to action. The nation was not being attacked nor was there any identifiable significance to it in terms that most Americans would understand. The enemy -- "The Gook" -- was hard to define; few knew where Korea was located and fewer still understood that it was divided not only into North and South, but into Eastern and Western influence in the cold war.

Korea was the first American "ideological war" as Knox described it. It was fought -- and a lot of men died -- strictly for an idea. It ended, if in fact one can really say that it has ended, with a compromise rather than a victory. It was a limited war fought by a nation that was not known for its ability to limit anything.

Yet this war which the United States came so close to losing, and was not allowed to win, was fought with caution designed to prevent the use of and spread of nuclear weapons. And with the full realization that at any time it could well be the beginning of World War III.

It was as uncertain an event as America wanted to have to deal with. Soldiers went, and most returned, without fanfare. And, unlike Vietnam, every effort was made to forget it as quickly as possible. Only now, long after monuments to intervening wars have been constructed, has a memorial to the Korean veteran been planned. And this only after years of effort by a few Korean veterans, rather than as a statement of interest or respect by the American people.

The official cost of this war to the American people was the death of 54,246 service persons, 103,248 wounded, and 5,178 missing in action. It cost about 67 billion dollars with at least another 10 billion in equipment left on the fields of combat to rust.

At 4:00 am on Sunday the 25th of June, 1950, some ninety thousand soldiers of the North Korean People's Army (NKPA) crossed the thirty-eighth parallel and began what President Truman was to label the Korean Conflict. This attacking army consisted of an armored brigade, seven infantry divisions, a specialized infantry regiment, a brigade of border constabulary, and a motorcycle regiment, supported by artillery and air support.

To stem this crushing tide the Republic of Korea (ROK) had four infantry divisions, only one regiment of each in defense. The remainder was located in rest and training areas some ten to forty miles south of the attack. Among these groups a large percentage of the men and officers were on pass.

Led by forty Soviet-built T-34 tanks, two divisions of the NKPA moved south through the Uijongbu Corridor heading for Seoul. By nightfall on the 25th the 7th ROK division, had retreated to the village of Uijongbu, and

were all that stood in the way of the nation's capital
at Seoul. Despite desperate efforts by the Republic of
Korean the NKPA overthrew Uijongbu and moved toward
Seoul. By Tuesday, 27 June 1950 the government of South
Korea abandoned its capital and by midnight of that day
the forward units of the NKPA reached Seoul.

At 2:15 in the morning of the 28th panicking
soldiers and engineers blew the last remaining hope of
the retreating army when it destroyed the Han River
bridges. Thousands of refugees were killed and nearly
forty thousand soldiers, and their badly needed
equipment, were trapped on the northern side of the
bridge. By nightfall on the 28th Seoul was in the hands
of the North Koreans, the ROK army was virtually
destroyed, and the American government was confused.

The United States, despite its involvement in the
creation of a North and South Korea, seemed to consider
it of very little military importance. The Joint Chiefs
of Staff virtually wrote it off in 1947. The United
Nations had accepted a mandate for elections in Korea
and, while those elections had led to violence and the
eventual definition of the North and the South along the
thirty-eighth parallel, it gave the United Nations a
sense of responsibility.

When word reached Washington of the North Korean
attack it was considered a probe, probably related to
Russian interests in Europe and maybe even to an attack
there. Also, diplomacy -- or perhaps it was the failure
of diplomacy -- had led the Communists to believe that
the United States was no more interested in defending
South Korea than it had been to interfere in the
Communist takeover of Nationalist China.

Harry S Truman was indecisive, but Secretary
General Trygve Lie of the United Nations declared it was
a "war against the United Nations" and called for an
immediate meeting of the UN Security Council. By 6:00
that evening the Council, with Russia absent following
a dramatic walkout some months before, adopted a
resolution condemning the North Koreans for a breach of
the peace and calling for cessation of the war, a
withdrawal to the thirty-eighth parallel, and for all
members of the UN to give no assistance to the North
Koreans.

Truman decided to act. Douglas MacArthur, World War II hero of the Pacific War, and military commander of the region, was ordered to send equipment and supplies, and to provide air and naval support to protect the delivery of these supplies. Also, to provide for the safe evacuation of American citizens. Within hours American jets stationed in Japan had clashed with Soviet-built Yak fighters and had destroyed them.

After a quick visit to the front on the 29th of June, MacArthur requested American combat forces; a regimental combat team to delay the North Koreans and a force of two divisions to follow up. President Truman agreed.

A Task Force under the command of Lt. Col. Charles B. Smith, and consisting of the 1st Battalion of the 21st Infantry Regiment of the 24th Infantry Division, was immediately airborne from garrison in Japan to Korea. The rest of the division was to follow as quickly as possible.

Task Force Smith, as it was to be known, entered the fight through Pusan on the 2nd of July. The Task Force set up defense along the road from Suwon to Osan. On 5 July, a line of Soviet-built tanks overwhelmed the confident Americans. A young man who was assigned to machine gun duty was the first of more than 50,000 Americans to die in Korea.

The Americans, generally garrison troops, had a less than adequate knowledge about their job, or their equipment, but made a supreme effort to stem the tide. However, by late afternoon on the 5th, it became acutely obvious that they could not hold. Lt. Colonel Smith ordered a retreat. Equipment, wounded men, and large segments of disoriented personnel were lost while the few remaining survivors managed to reach Osan. They found it occupied by enemy tanks. They finally reached American lines where Colonel Smith discovered he could only account for 250 of his Task Force. The American presence had hardly slowed the assault.

With Osan gone the next defensible point appeared to be Pyongtaek, some ten miles to the south. General Dean with the forward units of the 24th Division arrived in Korea and were thrown into battle. The Americans were unable to hold, however, and withdrew further south hoping to make a stand at the Kum river, a major geographical landmark which ran southwest across Korea.

As the retreat continued MacArthur committed General Walker and his Eighth Army. Almost immediately Walker's headquarters moved to Korea but the arrival of troops was still very slow. The North Koreans were not to be stopped, and Eighth Army was not in time to prevent the heavy North Korean attack along the Kum. On 14 July the North Korean broke through the lines of the 34th Infantry Regiment and in the next few days also collapsed the lines held by the 19th Regiment.

MacArthur was placed in command of the army of the Republic of Korea and all troops in Korea were united under a single United Nations command. It became necessary for what was now called the United Nations forces to withdraw again, this time to Taejon.

There on the 19th of July another desperate battle began. Despite heavy and heroic defense the United Nations troops were once again forced to withdraw and Taejon was lost. General Dean was lost (later it was learned he had been captured) in the action and General Church took command of the 24th Division.

By 21 July the North Korean 12th Division had captured Yongju and the drive south continued. General Walker, realizing the diminishing options to his forces, issued the "stand or die" order designed to change the American attitude of retreat. But retreat was necessary and again on August 1st and 2nd they withdrew behind the Naktong river and formed what was to be known as the Pusan Perimeter, a rectangle about 100 miles long north to south and about 50 miles east to west. The Naktong, flowing south, formed the western boundary. The northern flank was defended by the ROK, to the west the 1st Cavalry, the 24th and 25th Infantry Division, the 5th Regimental Combat Team and the almost 5000 troops of the 1st Provisional Marine Brigade (5th Marines) who were attached to the 25th Division.

An American counterattack, primarily to strengthen the Perimeter, was launched under the leadership of Task Force Kean between August 5th and 10th westward to recapture Chinju. For two weeks the battle raged, centering on Battle Mountain which changed hands so many times no one seems to know how many. Survivors identified these August battles as "the days along the Naktong" during which the North Korean commanders, aware that time was running against them, pushed harder and harder. Under these attacks the Pusan Perimeter shrank back another fifteen to twenty miles to the southeast where it held.

The vital Pusan-Kyongju-Taegu-Pusan railroad loop within the perimeter, which was run by engineers from the Army Transportation Corps, made the movement of troops and supplies possible. Slowly the American troops were receiving not only vital replacements, but supplies of the first order. The advantage of this internal system allowed Walker to move men quickly to damn up the hundreds of breakthrough pushed by the North Koreans along the line. The Perimeter allowed the United Nations Forces, still 95 per cent American, to establish a continuous line, build up, plan for attack, and hold on while their troop and supply situation improved.

A second Naktong offensive was launched by Walker and Church using the 5th Marines as point. The driving force met, and basically destroyed the 4th North Korean Division, but the effect was short lived as the 3rd North Korean Division attacked at Waegwan. MacArthur called on the B-29s for a bombed carpet to slow the enemy. But the intensity of the battle became nearly overwhelming in what has become known as "the Bowling Alley" where both sides met in five days of almost continuous combat. The conclusion was a slow withdrawal of the demoralized North Koreans and the American return to Masas.

It was the decision on an invasion at Inchon which was to finally mark the military reversal. Whether it turned the tide of the war and rescued the mauled Eighth Army is one of the questions still being addressed. There is considerable doubt if the North Korean army could have sustained any prolonged attack on Pusan and every evidence was that Walker, given a little time, could well have broken from the Perimeter and fought his way back up to the Korean thirty-eighth parallel.

On the last day of August the North Koreans, having assembled about 98,000 men, formed for what must have been seen as the last possible effort for success against the Perimeter.   Attacking early in September they broke through the American lines on several points, the Naktong Bulge being the greatest danger.   Walker counterattacked on the 4th and 5th of September but it did little to slow the North Koreans.

On the 5th the marines were ordered out of the line to prepare for their amphibious landing at Inchon and reflected the most dangerous point of the plan. Walker's staff was making plans for further retreat to the Davidson Line, the army's last-ditch defense, if necessary.   Any further retreat would recall a Dunkirk type evacuation.   Despite the danger and pressure on him, General "Bulldog" Walker decided to stay.

The success of the Inchon landing broke the heart of the North Korean troops pushing against Pusan.   It was not possible for the Eighth Army to move out on 16 September as planned -- apparently the North Korean troops there did not know of the attack against Inchon and the presence of an army at their rear.   But within the week the breakout of the Perimeter was accomplished and troops were moving to link up with the advanced section of 5th Marines and 7th Division heading inland toward the capital at Seoul.

CHRONOLOGY OF
SIGNIFICANT EVENTS

Korean War: (Known as the Korean Conflict until 1958
    when it was officially changed to the Korean War.)

1949

30 June   Last American occupation troops removed.

               Korean Military Assistance Group, a small
               unit of about 500 advisors, remained.

1950

18 June   John Foster Dulles, consultant to Dean
               Acheson, visited Seoul.

19 June   Acheson promised the Korean National
               Assembly "You are not alone."

25 June   North Korean Army invades the Republic of
               South Korea.

               Ambassador John J. Muccio reported "an all
               out offensive against the Republic" is under
               way.

US requests meeting of the UN Security Council.

UN Security Council (Soviet Union absent) meets. UN Resolution calls for cessation of hostilities.

President Truman authorizes General MacArthur to provide logistic aid to Republic of Korea.

Ambassador Muccio orders American dependents evacuated.

26 June   Republic of Korea appeals to UN for aid in stopping North Korea.

UN rejects North Korean assertions that South Korea attacked first.

26-27 June   Two thousand American dependents and other foreigners evacuated by sea and air.

27 June   President Truman orders US air and sea forces to provide cover and support to South Korea.

UN Security Council accepts US request for UN aid to repel North Korean attack and restore peace.

Four American fighters, covering evacuation, shot down three North Korean planes. Four more shot down later in the day.

North Korean radio called for the surrender of Seoul.

ROK Army headquarters deserted Seoul. South Korean army blows Han River bridges, trapping thousands in Seoul.

28 June   North Korean forces take and occupy Seoul.

29 June   General MacArthur flies to Korea to provide military evaluation.

President Truman identifies US presence in Korea as a police action. Planes of US Far East Air Forces flew 172 combat sorties in support of ROK Army.

American cruiser <u>Juneau</u> began shelling North Korean targets.

30 June   President Truman authorizes air attacks on North Korea, naval blockade of Korean coast, and the use of US ground troops in South Korea.

1 July   First US Troops (Task Force Smith) arrive in Korea.

North Korean Army sent its main force across the Han river heading for Yongdungpo.

2 July   US rejects Nationalist China's offer of 33,000 troops to be used in Korea.

3 July   Industrial city of Yongdungpo falls to North Korean troops.

Cruiser <u>Juneau</u> along with two British ships participated in an engagement with the North Korean Navy, sinking two torpedo boats and seven trawlers.

5 July   Task Force Smith engages North Korean Army near Osan.

First American killed.

6 July   American troops fight brief holding action at Pyongtaek, but quickly retreat.

7 July   UN authorizes unified UN Command for forces in Korea.

	General Walker (Eighth Army) visits Korea.
8 July	General MacArthur named as UN Commander.
	South Korean President Rhee puts ROK ground forces under General MacArthur's command.
12 July	US sets up defense line on the banks of the Kum River.
12-13 July	US troops cross Kum River.
13 July	General Walker named US troop commander in Korea: Eighth Army took over ground war.
14 July	North Korean troops move on Kongju area.
15 July	Kum River line broken.
16 July	North Korean troops cross Kum River.
18 July	US 1st Cavalry and 25th Infantry Divisions arrive in Korea.
19 July	North Korean troops penetrate defenses around Taejon.
20 July	UN Forces abandon Taejon.
20-21 July	General Dean captured by North Koreans.
24 July	North Korean attack near Sangyong delayed but US Forces retreat.
26 July	General Walker announced plan for strategic withdrawal into defensive line.
29 July	General MacArthur visits Eighth Army. Shortly after Walker reportedly orders "stand or die."
31 July	North Koreans take Chinju.

First Marines and 2nd Infantry arrive in Korea.

1 August   General Walker orders further withdrawal.

UN forces move into Pusan Perimeter.

6-8 August   MacArthur confers with Averell Harriman, and Generals Almond, Norstad, and Ridgway about possible landing at Inchon.

11 August   North Korean troops attack Yongsan.

14-16 Aug   UN counterattacks and hold North Koreans at Taegu.

15 August   Date set by North Korean Leader Kim Il Sung for victory over UN Forces.

19 August   Marines and 34th Infantry repel attack on "Naktong Bulge" shattering the North Korean 4th Division.

25 August   Reports received of Chinese Communist troops massing near the Korean border.

1-3 Sept   Major North Korean attacks on Pusan Perimeter countered, and forces held.

6 Sept   North Korean forces push to within six miles from Taegu.

7 Sept   Joint Chiefs of Staff request a re-evaluation of General MacArthur's Inchon plan.

12 Sept   Secretary of Defense Johnson's resignation is required by President Truman.

General George Marshall named Secretary of Defense.

13 Sept   Aerial and Naval bombardment began, concentrated at Wolmi-do.

15 Sept   UN Forces invade Inchon successfully.

18 Sept   UN Forces capture Kimpo Airfield.

28 Sept   UN Forces retake Seoul.

30 Sept   Republic of South Korea troops cross 38th Parallel.

THE PUSAN PERIMETER, KOREA, 1950

ARCHIVES AND DOCUMENTS

Archival Materials

Combined Arms Research Library, United States Command
and General Staff College (Fort Leavenworth)
USAF Airborne Operations, World War II and Korea
War [Official use only].

Defense Audiovisual Agencies, Still Photographic
Depository, No. 168 (Anacostia Naval Station,
Washington)
Still photography Korean War Period.

Dwight D. Eisenhower Presidential Library (Abilene)
Dwight D. Eisenhower (Pre-presidential) Papers,
1916-1952.

Federal Records Center (Kansas City)
KMAG: A General File, 1949-1950.

Harry S Truman Presidential Library (Independence)
  Dean Acheson papers
  Eben Ayers
  Matthew Connelly
  William Draper
  George M. Elsey
  John F. Melby
  John H. Muccio, oral histories
  Frank Pace
  Harold Smith
  John Summers
  Harry S Truman

Hoover Institute on War Stanford University
    (Stanford)
  Miscellaneous File, Korea, Accession TS Korea U58
  North Korean Propaganda materials

MacArthur Memorial Bureau of Archives (Norfolk)
  Messages between MacArthur and the Joint Chiefs
  General Headquarters, UN Command, 1945-1951,
    USAF in Korea

Modern Military Records Branch, National Archives
    (Washington)
  Official Reports Eighth Army, tactical narrative
    section of the monthly command reports I, IX, X
    corps as well as the six combat divisions and 19
    regiments.
  Military History Section of Headquarters, Far East
    Command, "History of the Korean War, Chronology,
    25 June 1950 - 31 December 1951", 25th Division,
    Record Group 407, 3rd Division, Record Group 407.
  National Security Council.
  Roy Appleman's collection of letters and comments
    from participants in the Korean War.
  Messages between the Joint Chiefs of Staff and
    General Headquarters in Tokyo, Record Group 218.
    Most of these are published in Foreign Relations
    of the United States, volume 7, 1951.

Army Plans and Operations Division, Record Group 319.

Department of the Army, Record Group 336.

Office of the Secretary of Defense, Record Group 330.

"Record of Actions Taken by the Joint Chiefs of Staff Relative to the United Nations Operations in Korea from 25 June 1950 to 11 April 1951, Prepared by Them", 107 pages.

Intelligence Summaries, North Korean, Record Group 739.

Intelligence (G-2) Library, United States Army, Record Group 319.

Unit Histories
These hard to locate "official" histories are generally by amateurs, more pictures than text, but very helpful. They include:

1st Cavalry	24th Division
2nd Cavalry	25th Division
3rd Division	89th Tank Battalion
7th Division	187th Airborne

The manuscripts of several unpublished unit histories are also on file,
G. Bittman Barth "Tropic Lightning and Taro Leaf"
Paschall and Mary Strong "Sabers and Safety Pins"
G. C. Stewart "My Service During the Korea War"
James H. Dill "Diary and Personal Adventures"

The National Archives, Federal Records Center
(Suitland)
Far Eastern Command, Record Group 332.
Far East Command "Chinese Communist Military Operations in Korea", Record Group 407.
Supreme Commander for the Allied Powers, Records Group 331.
War Diaries (to 1 December 1950) Record Group 407.
War Diaries, staff section journals, unit journals, periodic operation reports, operation instruction, telephone logs, map overlays, 24th Infantry Division, 34th Regiment.

1st Provisional Brigade, United States Marine Corps, are housed at Suitland but remain under the control of the Historical Branch USMC.

Historical Reports, United States Military Advisors Group to the Republic of Korea (KMAG) 1949-1950.

Files relating to Roy Appleman <u>South to the Naktong, North to the Yalu</u> and Lynn Montross and Nicholas Canzona <u>The Pusan Perimeter</u> as official publications.

<u>National Personnel Records Center, Military Personnel Records</u> (St. Louis)

Military personnel (201) files.

<u>Naval Historical Center, Office of Navy History</u> (Washington)

General Headquarters, Tokyo, <u>History of the North Korean Army</u>.

<u>Office of the Chief of Military History</u> (Washington)

Orientation Folder, General William L. Roberts, 1950.

<u>Still Picture Division, Main Archives</u> (Washington)

Still photographs of the Korean War.

<u>United Nations Archives</u> (Washington)

<u>United Nations Documents, 1946-1960</u>. Readex Microprint Edition. Readex, New York: Microprint Corporation, 1978. Thousands of microfiche records and primary documents housed under separate headings for the General Assembly, Atomic Energy Commission, United Nations Administrative Tribunal, Disarmament Commission, Economic and Social Council, Security Council, United Nations Special Fund Governing Council, and Trustee Council. Military, as well as diplomatic efforts by the United States in the United Nations is

apparent in these documents which, if used, require extensive work in the indexes, which are separately housed and on microfiche.

United States Army Military History Institute
(Carlisle Barracks, Pennsylvania)
Oral History Collection
Edward M. Almond
Mark W. Clark
Frank Pace
Matthew B. Ridgway
Maxwell D. Taylor

U. S. Marine Corps History (Division) Museum
(Navy Yard, Washington)
Oral History Reports
  Alpha A. Bowser
  Edward A. Craig
  Oliver P. Smith
  Gerald C. Thomas
Diary File (Battalions) First Marine Division

Published Documents

Congressional Record

001   Ammunition Shortages in the Armed Services
Congressional Record, Senate, 83rd Congress, 1st session, 1953.
     A look at the early shortages of appropriate ammunition for the Armed Forces. The problems being more related to the right ammunition than the total supply.

002 <u>Hearings on the Military Situation in the Far East</u> Congressional Record, Senate, 82nd Congress, 1st session, 1951.

Voluminous collection of testimony concerning the military situation, United States and United Nation objectives and General MacArthur's release from command.

003 <u>The Korean War and Related Matters</u> Congressional Record, Senate, 84th Congress, 1st session, 1955.

A wrap-up look at the war and the consequences of American involvement. Very general, most materials available in other sources.

004 <u>The United States and the Korean Problem, Documents, 1943-1953</u>. Congressional Record, Senate, 1953.

A collection of documents relating to the United States role in Korea, occupation, KMAG, and the Korean War years.

Department of State Publications

BOOKS

005 <u>American Foreign Policy: Basic Documents, 1950-1955, Part XV, Korea</u>. Washington, DC: Department of State Publications, 1957.

Basic documents of the outbreak, policy development and execution of the Korean War. Primarily document pages 2527-2738.

006 <u>The Conflict in Korea: Events Prior to the Attack on June 25, 1950</u>. Department of State Publication Far Eastern Studies 4266, (October 1951). 36 pages.

Gives the diplomatic and legal background of the United States commitment to Korea. Heavily used by Appleman in his official history <u>South to the Naktong, North to the Yalu</u>. Very important collection of materials about American involvement and why the United States was willing to go to war at this time and under these circumstances.

007   Department of Defense. <u>Semi-annual Reports of the</u>
<u>Secretary of Defense, and Semi-annual Reports of the</u>
<u>Secretary of the Army, Secretary of the Navy, Secretary</u>
<u>of the Air Force, January 1 to June 30 and July 1 to</u>
<u>December 30, 1950 through 1953</u>. Washington,   DC:
Government Printing Office, 1950-1955.
      These reports on military action are filed by field
and theater commanders, including reports from both
Eighth Army and Far East Command, during the period of
the Pusan Perimeter defense.

008   Department of State. <u>United States Policy in the</u>
<u>Korean Conflict, July 1950-February 1951</u>. Publication
Number 4263.
      Analysis of governmental policy leading to the
Korean Conflict, the period of decision, and United
States relations to the United Nations during the first
year.

009   <u>Foreign Relations of the United States 1950</u>.
Volume 7   "Korea"   Washington, DC: Government Printing
Office, 1972.
      Contains important documents relating to the
outbreak of the Korean War and the decision for
intervention.   Deals with some of the more important
"behind the scene" pressures and decisions.

010   <u>Foreign Relations of the United States 1950</u>.
Volume 7 "Korea" Washington, DC: Department of State
Publications, Office of the Historian, 1976.
      Eighth Army Commander reports, Joint Chiefs Policy
#99935, 2 January 1951.   Plans drawn to complete a
withdrawal if it becomes necessary, policy statement for
withdrawal and the conditions under which permission is
given.   Deals primarily with early Korean questions.

011   <u>Foreign Relations of the United States 1951</u>.
Volume 7 "Korea and China" Parts One and Two,
Washington, DC: Government Printing Office, 1983.
      Primarily copies of reports and documents dealing
with the first full year of the war in Korea.

012   Records of the Joint Chiefs of Staff; Part I,
Meetings of the Joint Chiefs of Staff, 1946-1953.
Frederick, Maryland: University Publication, 1980.
     Minutes of the meetings of the Joint Chiefs during
the Korean War, especially useful in considering both
the military view of why the United States was involved
and how it fought the first period. Microfilm available
in 8 reels. Declassified in 1970.

013   Records of the Joint Chiefs of Staff; Part II, The
Far East, 1946-1953. Frederick, Maryland: University
Publication, 1980.
     Documents of military activities and policies
during the pre-war Korean involvement, the invasion and
American military reaction, as well as the first year of
defense.   Very helpful in trying to understand the
military mind, the policy of involvement, and how the
war was to be fought. Microfilm available in 14 reels.

014   U. S. Policy in the Korean Crisis, 1950.
Department of State Publication 3922, Far East Series
34. Washington, DC: Government Printing Office, 1950.
     Messages which established policy and American
involvement.

                        ARTICLES

015   "Act of Aggression in Korea" Department of State
Bulletin 23 (July 10, 1950) 43-46.
     In an address to the American Newspaper Guild,
Secretary Acheson reports that all actions taken in
Korea have been under the aegis of the United Nations.

016   "Aims and Objectives in Resisting Aggression in
Korea" Department of State Bulletin 23 (September 11,
1950) 407-410.
     An address by President Truman from the White
House, 1 September 1950 during which he talks to the
American people about why the United States is in Korea,
and what the objectives are.   What is at stake is
liberty, ours and theirs.

017   "Charging South Korea as Aggressor Reminiscent of
Nazi Tactics"   Department of State Bulletin   23 (July
17, 1950) 87.
      Statement by Secretary Acheson indicates that a
free nation knows the truth (of who is responsible for
the war) and is not going to be misled by false versions
of it.

018   Muccio, John J. "Korea and the Explosion of a
Communist Delusion" Department of State Bulletin 26
(June 16, 1952) 939-942.
      Discusses the victories won in the Korean War,
meaning first, the prevention of a communist state with
the division of North and South Korea and United Nations
elections; and second, the victory following Inchon.

019   "Review of Security Council Action in Defense of
Korea"   Department of State Bulletin 23 (September 18,
1950) 451-454.
      An address by Ambassador Warren R. Austin broadcast
on CBS 31 August 1950 on the need for military action by
the United Nations to prevent a communist victory in
Korea.

020   Special Report of UN Commanding General. "Captured
Documents" Department of State Bulletin 24 (May 21,
1951) 828-830.
      Includes the two captured documents, presented to
the United Nations as evidence by the American
government, which clearly show the North Korean forces
were ordered to attack.

021   Truman, Harry S. "Preventing a New World War"
Department of State Bulletin 24 (April 16, 1951) 603-
605.
      Text of President Truman's 11 April 1951, 10:30 pm
address to the nation in which he explains that the
decision to enter the Korean Conflict was a good one,
and that it was the only decision to prevent World War
III.

022   US Department of State. "White Paper on Korea"
Current History 19 (1950) 170-174.
    On 4 July 1950, Deputy Foreign Minister Gromyko
blamed the United States for the hostilities. This is
the official reply which, after tracing the post-World
War II history, blames North Korean aggression and
stresses the fact the United States is responding to
United Nations pressure.

Official Military Sources

BOOK

023   American Forces in Action. 14 Pamphlets.
Washington, DC. Government Printing Office, 1943-1947.
    Popular printing pamphlets designed to show the
locations and actions of American fighting forces.
Among those considered is the occupation and first year
of military government in Korea.

ARTICLES

024   Baya, G. Emery. "Army Organization Act of 1950"
Army Information Digest 5:8 (1950) 28-37.
    This reflects the organization of the army as it
operated throughout the war.   Signed into law by
President Truman just three days after the North Korean
invasion,   it   consolidated   several   previous
organizational laws, and was the military configuration
from which the war was fought.

025   Doughty, Robert.   "The Evolution of U. S. Army
Tactical Doctrine, 1946-1976" Leavenworth Papers:
Combat Study Series Institute. Leavenworth, Kansas: US
Army Command and General Staff College, 1979. 57 pages.
    Discusses the development of tactical doctrines
through the post-World War II era. Chapter seven deals
with the Korean period, and is primarily concerned with
shortages in unit size and limited supply and equipment.

026   "Pertinent   Papers   on   the   Korean   Situation"
Executive Branch: Documents and Reports. 8 volumes,
United States Department of Defense: Office of Joint
Chiefs of Staff, 1953. Mimeographed.

No compiler is listed for this rather extensive
collection of materials which consists of documents
concerning the American and United Nations decision to
enter the war, and the early fighting. Very incomplete.

027 Ridgway, Matthew B. "The Korean War, Issues and
Policies" Manuscript, Center of Military History,
Washington, DC. 360+ pages.

A book length document developed by General Ridgway
concerning the political, as well as military, aspects
of fighting the Korean War.   This manuscript has been
used extensively by Billy C. Mossman in Ebb and Flow,
but is available for further research.

United Nations Report

ARTICLE

028 "Analysis of Issues by Korean Commission"
United Nations Bulletin 9 (October 1, 1950) 301-304.

United Nations Commission lists the North Korean
invasion as "an act of aggression initiated without
warning and without provocation."

SECONDARY SOURCES

Bibliographies, Dictionaries, and References

BOOKS

029 American University. <u>U.S. Army Handbook for Korea</u>. Washington, DC: Government Printing Office, 1958.
     This handbook was prepared for American servicemen who were being sent to Korea. It is a quick, but good, reference to the history, politics, and culture of both Koreas.

030   <u>The Army Almanac</u>.   Harrisburg: The Stackpole Company, 1959.   797 pages, name and topic indexes.
     Basic facts concerning the organization and management of the United States Army.   The army was reorganized in 1949, a reorganization which was tested in the early days of the Korean War.

031   Association of Asian Studies. <u>Cumulative Bibliography of Asian Studies 1941-1965; Subject Bibliography</u>. 4 Volumes. Boston: Hall, 1970-1972.
     Volumes three and four of this carefully collected bibliography contain numerous articles dealing with the Korean War. These sections are all of works available in English. Lack of an index makes it very hard to use.

032 Bibliography of Social Science Periodicals and
Monograph Series Republic of Korea, 1945-1961.
Washington, DC: Superintendent of Documents, US
Government Printing Office, 1962. Foreign Bibliography
Series, P-92, No. 9, iv-48 pages.
    A selected bibliography of articles and monographs
dealing with Korea during the period from the American
occupation through the war. Some deal with Pusan.

033 Blanchard, Carroll H. Jr. An Atlas of the War in
Korea, 1950 - 1953, Volume 2. The Pusan Perimeter.
Albany, New York: State University of New York, 1992.
    Maps drawn or collected by Blanchard give a
detailed and easy picture of the fighting lines, troop
placement, the movement of fronts, and occupied
territory at any given time.

034 Blanchard, Carroll H. Jr. Korean War Bibliography
and Maps of Korea. Albany, New York: Korean Conflict
Research Foundation, 1964. Subject and author index.
    The first publication of a very ambitious program
to collect and identify all materials dealing with the
War. His subject arrangements are somewhat difficult
but he has identified some materials that do not appear
elsewhere. Good but thirty years old.

035 Chung, Yong Sun. (compiler). Korean: A Selected
Bibliography, 1959-1963. Kalamazoo, Michigan: Korean
Research and Publications, 1965.
    The title is confusing, apparently meaning works
published during those dates, for it does contain more
than fifty works on the war itself. These materials
include some North Korean sources and are generally
available in English.

036 Coletta, Paolo E. (compiler). A Bibliography of
American Naval History. Annapolis, Maryland: Navy
Institute, 1981.
    This massive listing of works on naval history
includes not only articles, books, monographs but theses
and dissertations as well. More than a hundred of these
works are on the Korean War, a few which relate to the
first six months.

037   Edwards, Paul M. (compiler). <u>General Matthew B.</u>
<u>Ridgway: A   Bibliography</u>.   Westport,   Connecticut:
Greenwood Press, 1993. 135 pages, index.
      An up-to-date work from a knowledgeable historian
of the Korean War. This work is part of the Greenwood
Press <u>Battles and Leaders Series</u> and covers the life of
General Ridgway who was involved as Assistant Chief of
Staff, Joint Chiefs. A good reference in understanding
the climate before and after the Korean War.   It
includes multiple sources and references to the Pusan
Perimeter. See index.

038   Eggenberger, David. <u>A Dictionary of Battles</u>. New
York: Crowell, 1967. 526 pages, bibliography.
      Describes key battles from 1460 BC to 1966,
including a few from the Korean conflict. Provides some
descriptions of the location, major causes for the
conflict, and military commanders engaged.

039   Greenwood, John. (compiler). <u>American Defense</u>
<u>Policy   Since   1945:   A   Preliminary   Bibliography</u>.
Lawrence, Kansas: University Press of Kansas, 1973.
      Lists sixty or so works on the outbreak and early
political considerations of the Korean War. A good
solid collection, but greatly limited by the lack of an
index.

040   Imperial War Museum Library. <u>The War in Korea,</u>
<u>1950-1953, A List of Selected References</u>. London: War
Museum Library, 1961.
      This mimeographed list produced by the British,
includes more than 350 books, articles, and monographs
in English on the Korean War. It includes references to
both British and American units.

041   <u>Key Korean War Battles Fought in the Republic of</u>
<u>Korea</u>. APO, San Francisco: Headquarters, Eighth United
States Army, 1972.
      A short and very one sided account of the
significant battles fought by United States Eighth Army
in Korea during the Korean War.

042 McFarland, Keith D. The Korean War: An Annotated Bibliography. New York: Garland Publishers, 1986. 461 pages, subject and author index.

An excellent collection of materials dealing with the war, well arranged and easy to identify, cross referenced in index. The annotations are brief but crisp. In his citation he does not identify indexes in individual works. Other than the fact so many new materials have appeared since 1986, this is a fine and useful research tool.

043 Matray, James I. (editor). Historical Dictionary of the Korean War. Westport, Connecticut: Greenwood Press, 1991. 648 pages, index, photographs, maps, bibliography.

Provides a useful tool to assist in understanding the war, describes significant people, controversies, military operations, and policy. Good for the occasional reference to minor operations.

044 O'Quinlivan, Michael and James S. Santelli. An Annotated Bibliography of the United States Marines in the Korean War. Washington, DC: Historical Branch G-3 Division, Headquarters US Marines, 1962. Revised 1970.

A good but dated listing of materials dealing with the United States Marine Corps action during the Korean War. Annotations very limited.

045 Park, Hong-Kyu. The Korean War: An Annotated Bibliography. Marshall, Texas: Demmer Co., Inc., 1971. 29 pages.

A brief and very selective work which concentrates on Korean entries (in English). Limited and dated.

046 A Revolutionary War: Korea and the Transformation of the Postwar World. Colorado Springs, Colorado: USAF Academy Library, Special Bibliography Series, No. 84, October 1992.

A brief but informative bibliography directed toward support of the idea the Korean War was more revolutionary than international.

047   Schuon,   Karl.   U.S. Marine Corps Biographical
Dictionary.   New   York: Watts,   1963.   278   pages,
photographs.
      Select brief sketches of officers and enlisted
men, many of whom distinguished themselves during the
early fighting in Korea.

048   Summers, Harry G. Jr.   Korean War Almanac.   New
York: Facts   on   File,   1990.   330   pages,   index,
photographs, maps, bibliography.
      Brief but informative coverage of major events, and
personalities. A useful tool in bringing other works up
to date.

049   Thursfield, Henry G. (editor).   Brassey's Annual:
The Armed Forces Year Book, 1950 - 1954.   New York:
Macmillan, 1950 - 1954.
      A good collection, most helpful because of its
listings of both British and Commonwealth units in
action during the Korean Conflict.

050 Traverso, Edmund.   Korea and the Limits of Limited
War. Menlo Park, California: Addison-Wesley Publishers,
1970.   81 pages.
      Primarily a source book for documents dealing with
the concept of limited war, a policy which was first
invoked in Korea.   Helpful to locate primary materials
which reflect the move toward American involvement.

051 United Nations Efforts Against Aggression in Korea,
Bibliography. Washington, DC: Library of Congress, n.d.
      A limited bibliography directed by the assumption
of North Korean acts of aggression.   Concerned with
works which support the idea the Korean War was the
result of communist aggression in South Korea.

052   United States Department of the Army. Communist
North Korea: A Bibliographic Survey. Washington, DC:
Government Printing Office, 1962.
      A very selective bibliographical source on the
communist government and troops in North Korea.

053   <u>Webster's   American   Military   Biographies</u>.
Springfield, Massachusetts: Merriam, 1978.
     Contains numerous brief sketches of military
leaders who served in the early years of the Korean
conflict.

ARTICLES

054   Lee, Chong-Sik. "Korea and the Korean War" in
Thomas Hammond. (editor). <u>Soviet Foreign Relations and
World Communism</u>. Princeton: Princeton University Press,
1965. 787-806.
     Contains nearly fifty works on the Korean War, most
of them on the larger political issues.   Very well
annotated.

055   Paige, Glenn D.   "A Survey of Soviet Publications
on Korea, 1950 - 1956"   <u>Journal of Asian Studies</u>
(August 7, 1958)   579-594.
     For the serious student this provides a look at how
the war was covered and analyzed by the Russian
government and intellectual community.

056   Saunders, Jack. "Records in the National Archives
Relating to Korea 1945-1950" Bruce Cumings. (editor)
<u>Child of Conflict</u>.   Seattle, Washington: University of
Washington Press, 1983.   309-326.
     This essay provides an excellent guide to materials
that have become available concerning the Korean War.
The declassification has come about through the use of
the Freedom of Information Act.

057   "The War in Korea -- A Chronology of Events, 25
June 1950 - 25 June 1951"   <u>World Today</u> 7:8 (1951) 317-
328.
     A day by day account of the various political and
military events of the first year. It is very helpful
to the student who is trying to work out the order of
the fast moving events leading to, and during, the
period of the Pusan Perimeter.

058 "The War in Korea: Diaries for June 25 - July 30, 1950; August 1 - October 31, 1950" Royal United Service Institute Journal 95 486-491, 601-611; and 96 148-155, 298-305.
     British orientation to the day by day activities of the war, accounting for the first four months.

059 Warner, Geoffrey. "The Korean War" International Affairs 56:1 (1980) 98-107.
     Fifteen bibliographical essays written by historians of the British Commonwealth which look at the question of who is to blame for the starting of the war. While these historians are no more able to determine the cause and fault than are others, the essays are better than average, especially in looking at leaders of the various factions.

Historiographic

BOOK

060 Making Known the Korean War: Policy Analysis of the Korean Conflict in the Last Decade. Unknown publisher, date.
     An overview of historiographic trends in considering the Korean War policies and analysis during the 1980s. Listed in several bibliographies, and listed at the Command and Staff College Library.

ARTICLES

061 Leopold, Richard W. "The Korean War: The Historian's Task" Francis H. Heller. (editor) The Korean War: A 25-Year Perspective. Lawrence: The Regents Press of Kansas, 1977. 209-224.
     A dated but very good statement which addresses the lack of historical perspective concerning the Korean War. While Leopold makes a good case, the production of some fine Korean War history would seem to lessen the impact of his remarks. His general perspective, as well as his footnotes, are very helpful.

062 West, Philip. "Interpreting the Korean War" The American Historical Review 94 (February, 1989) 80-96.
     This is a combined review of six major Korean War books which Philip West identified suggesting, -- taking a phrase from Arthur Schlesinger, Jr., -- that the war has moved from the "heroic stage to the academic stage". He views the revisionist writings of the war premature as the real sources of information, North Korean and Chinese sources, are still very limited.

Prelude to War

Involvement Prior to the Conflict

ARTICLES

063 Cho, Soon-sung. "The Failure of American Military Government in Korea" Korean Affairs 2:3 (1963).
     Maintains that both the United States and Russia dealt with Korea independently, the American failure being that it left Korea with no clear governmental control and in the midst of chaos. The expectations of these two powers were unclear, thus led to irrational actions.

064 "The Conflict in Korea: Events Prior to the Attack on June 25, 1950" Department of State Far Eastern Studies 45 (1951).
     Discussion of the international political events, in which America was involved, which preceded the North Korean invasion of the South.

065 Sho, Kin Chull. "The Role of the Soviet Union in Preparation for the Korean War" Journal of Korean Affairs 3 (January 1974) 3-14.
     This article argues it was Russian training and equipment which made it possible for North Korea to launch an attack. Without this assistance there would have been no invasion.

066   "United States Policy in the Korean Crisis"   Far
Eastern Studies 34 (July 1950).
     Early collection on American policy during the
crisis in Korea. Deals primarily with policy making and
decisions, offering little on other aspects of the war.

KMAG

BOOKS

067 Historical Report. U. S. Military Advisory Group to
the Republic of Korea. (KMAG) Tokyo: Daito Art Printing
Company, Limited, Public Information Office. 1 July 1949
to 31 December 1949.
     Report of the Korean Military Advisory Group during
the effort to build up an ROK army. Though this troop
was left to prepare the ROK to defend itself, the lack
of both clarity and commitment in a policy toward Korea
is reflected in the limited success enjoyed.

068 KMAG, Public Information Office. The United States
Advisory Group to the Republic of Korea, 1945-1955.
Tokyo: Diate, n. d.
     Primarily an administrative history of the advisory
group responsible for the organization of the South
Korean armed forces, following KMAG from it conception
and taking it through the early fighting (where its
success proved doubtful) and on to their post-war role
The history is constrained and it tends to make too
strong a case for the benevolent nature of the advisors.

069 Sawyer, Robert K. and Walter G. Hermes. Military
Advisors in Korea: KMAG in Peace and War. Washington,
DC: Office of the Chief of Military History, Department
of the Army, 1962.
     The best book on the work of the Korean Military
Assistance Group, the primary military advisors in
Korea. This small force, left behind when the
occupation troops of the 7th Division were pulled out,
had the responsibility of training the army of the
Republic of Korea. How well they did their job, and the
limitations they faced in doing it, is discussed in this
short collection.

070   Sawyer, Robert K.   The Military Advisory Group to the Republic of Korea.   Volume I (September 1, 1945 - June 30, 1949). Volume II (July 1, 1949 to June 24, 1950). Volume III (June 25, 1950 to July 30, 1951). Manuscript in the Office of the Chief of Military History file.
    The material provided is basically the same as that in the published edition, but deals with the Advisory Group in more detail.

ARTICLES

071   Hall, Thomas A. "KMAG and the 7th ROK Division" Infantry 79:16 (November - December, 1989) 18-23, photos.
    This   previously   unavailable   and   unpublished material provided the daily journal of KMAG at Uijongbu during those difficult and intense days of 25-26 June, 1950.

072 Skroch, Ernest J. "Quartermaster Advisors in Korea" Quartermaster Review 31 (1951) 8-9, 118-123.
    Describes   the   activities   of   the   Quartermaster section of the Korean Military Advisory Group.   This section was responsible for establishing the ROK systems for the development of food supplies during the early war.

073 "Too Little, 45 Days Too Late" Collier's 126 (1950) 24-25.
    Maintains that United States leaders should have had no doubts of an attack since the South Korean Defense Minister had given the warning 45 days prior to the war. American leaders are thus responsible for the deaths of so many servicemen.

Invasion

BOOKS

074 Cumings, Bruce. The Roaring of the Cataract, 1947-1950. Princeton, New Jersey: Princeton University Press, 1981.
Very critical of the United States and appears to accept, with limited investigation, the Russian actions and intentions, but is rather fair in that the author finally accuses all nations for the outbreak of war in Korea.

075 Fleming, D. Frank. The Cold War and Its Origins, 1917-1960. Volume 2. Garden City, New York: Doubleday, 1961. 1158 pages.
This well researched work identifies the South Korean government as the primary cause of the outbreak of war.

ARTICLES

076 "Data for a Pearl Harbor Echo: Did We Muff It in Korea?" Newsweek 36 (July 10, 1950) 26-29.
Two days of super-secret hearings by the Senate Appropriations Committee draw startling admissions from General Lemnitzer, and John H. Ohly of the Mutual Defense Assistance, basically stating that America was uninformed, and unprepared. A concept which keeps coming up, but is never really answered.

077 DeWeerd, Harvey A. "Strategic Surprise in the Korean War" Position Paper (p-1800-L) RAND Corporation Paper, June 1962, Leavenworth, Kansas: US Army Command and Staff College Library. 35 pages.
Critical look at the failure of the United States intelligence prior to the outbreak of the Korean War. Cites information which should have shown an invasion was coming. Printed, with variation, in Orbis, 1962.

078   DeWeerd, Harvey A. "Strategic Surprise in Korea"
<u>Orbis</u> 6 (Fall 1962) 435-452.
    This RAND Corporation thinker admits that the pre-
war intelligence about the invasions was as bad as pre-
Pearl Harbor.   He suggests that the failure of
intelligence agencies to predict either the North Korean
or communist invasions may well have been a blessing in
disguise.   Now, at least, there is information about
how to handle such a crisis if it occurs again.

079   "Free Koreans Meet the Test of Battle" <u>Army
Information Digest</u> 5 (1950) 25-31.
    A pictorial account of the contribution made by the
South Koreans during the early months of the fighting,
and the toll taken upon the civilians as the army rushed
into retreat.

080   Gupta, Karunakar. "How Did the Korean War Begin?"
<u>China Quarterly</u> 52 (October/December 1972) 699-716.
    A well thought out discussion of the events
leading to war, the outbreak via "invasion", and an
analysis of the various "invasion theories."

081   "United States Far East Command, History of the
North Korean Army" Tokyo: G-2 Section, 1952. Manuscript.
    An attempt to trace the origins, the table of
organization and equipment, as well as the political
force behind the North Korean People's Army.

Responsibility for the War

BOOKS

082 Khrushchev, Nikita. <u>Khrushchev Remembers</u>. Boston:
Little, 1970. 639 pages, photographs.
    In these memoirs the Soviet Premier denies any
Russian involvement and claims Kim Il Sung was the
initiator. Should be read with considerable caution as
the authenticity has been questioned by some scholars.

083 Oliver, Robert T. <u>Why War Came In Korea</u>. New York:
Fordham University Press, 1950. 260 pages.
    Primarily an expanded version of his article of the
same name. It is a very critical look at United States
policy concerning Korea and finds that policy, and its
execution, to be stupid and bewildering. The message it
was sending to the Russians, as well as other nations,
was primarily responsible for the outbreak.

084 <u>Who Started the War?   The Truth About The Korean
Conflict</u>. Seoul: The Public Relations Association of
Korea, 1973.
    Provided with expected lack of objectivity this
"official" work identifies the North Korean government
who, with the aid of the Soviets, is blamed for a
totally unwarranted attack on the South.

ARTICLES

085 Cho, Li San. "Kim Started War" <u>The New York Times</u>
(July 6, 1990) A5.
    Li San Cho, the former North Korean ambassador,
says Kim Il Sung invented border incidents in order to
provide an excuse for the outbreak of war in 1950.

086 Crofts, Alfred. "The Start of the Korean War
Reconsidered" <u>Rocky Mountain Social Science Journal</u> 1
(1970) 109-117.
    Claims the causes of the war were indigenous to
Korea and the Koreans rather than some failure of
national policy either by the United States or Russia.

087 "Gromyko Statement" <u>Current History</u> 19 (September
1950) 167-174.
    Text of the 4 July 1950 statement by Russian
Foreign Minister Andrei Gromyko in which he charges the
United States with aggression; includes the "White
Paper."

088   Gye-Dong, Kim. "Who Initiated the Korean War?"
James Cotton and Ian Neary. (editors). The Korean War in
History. Atlantic Highlands, New Jersey: Humanities
Press International, 1989. 33-50.
      North Korea had the support of China and Russia in
making the decision, and they certainly were the
invaders, but the United States -- and to some degree
the United Nations -- were also to blame.

089   Halliday, Jon. "The Korean War: Some Notes on
Evidence and Solidarity" Bulletin of Concerned Asian
Scholars 3 (November 1979) 2-18.
      A British historian tries to make sense out of the
conflicting charges as to who is responsible for the
outbreak of the war. He finds the Western explanations
less than convincing. This author identifies the United
States as primarily to blame for the beginning of the
Korean War.   Makes the same argument as Riley and
Schram's The Reds Take a City. (see 221).

090   Hitchcock, Wilbur W. "North Korea Jumps the Gun"
Current History 20 (March 1951) 136-144.
      The   author   claims North Korea started the
aggression without Russian knowledge or approval, and
that Truman over-reacted to what was assumed to be the
start of World War III.

091   Oliver, Robert T. "Why War Came in Korea" Current
History 19 (1950) 139-143.
      This well known scholar has put together a rather
complicated case for the invasion based, in the largest
part, on Russian desires for an expansion of influences,
and on the United States failure to define a Korean
policy.

092   "United States Submits 'Conclusive Proof' of
Captured Army Orders" United Nations Bulletin 10 (June
15, 1951) 578-579.
      Provides what the United States displayed as their
"documented proof" that the North Koreans planned and
executed the attack on South Korea.

Decision for US and UN Involvement

BOOKS

093 Collins, J. Lawton. War in Peacetime. Boston: Houghton-Mifflin, 1969. 416 pages, index, photographs, map.

This book, by the man who served as Chief of Staff (Army) throughout the war, is most helpful for its initial discussion of the early decision to be militarily involved, the details of the Eighth Army retreat and finally the defense of Pusan. See chapter one - five, especially 100-113.

094 Detzer, David. Thunder of the Captains: The Short Summer in 1950. New York: Crowell, 1977. 243 pages, index, photographs, bibliography.

A narrative account of events in America and Korea, during the early summer of 1950, which eventually led to the United States decision to interfere. Popular account with strong personnel sketches.

095 Donovan, Robert J. Nemesis: Truman and Johnson in the Coils of War in Asia. New York: St. Martin's Press, 1984. 216 pages, index, photographs, notes.

An interesting comparison of presidential crises which had the unique characteristics of being totally misunderstood. Deals with the political climate, particularly, but has excellent discussion of the effect of the UN response, as well as certain key failures to respond, and on the retreat and final defense of Pusan. 79-84.

096 Goodrich, Leland M. Korea: A Study in U. S. Policy in the United Nations. New York: Council on Foreign Relations, 1956. 235 pages, photographs, appendix.

Careful handling of the Korean question in the United Nations from V-J Day to the Armistice in Korea. Particularly interesting in regards to UN versus American political interests.

097   Guttman, Allen. Korea and the Theory of Limited War. USA: D. C. Heath, 1967. 118 pages, essays.
      Primarily designed for a class in decision making, this collection contains key documents for understanding the outbreak of the war. Primary in importance is the UN Security Council Resolution, 27 June 1950 (2) and the text of Harry S Truman's "Our Aims in Korea" (13-14); other equally interesting documents are available here in print.

098   Paige, Glenn D. (compiler). 1950: Truman's Decision; The United States Enters The Korean War. New York: Chelsea, 1970. 177 pages, bibliography.
      A good companion to his work The Korean Decision. This is a significant collection of primary documents released prior to July 1, 1950 concerning the intervention decision.

099   Paige, Glenn D. The Korean Decision: June 24 - 30, 1950. New York: The Free Press, 1968. 419 pages, index.
      Probably the best work on the Truman intervention policy. Information which is taken from the official documents is re-enforced by interviews with participants from the State Department and the military who were involved in the decision. Looks at the unbelievable optimism of the Korean Military Advisory Group, and America's serious underestimation of the enemy.

100   Stairs, Denis. The Diplomacy of Constraint: Canada, the Korean War and the United States. Toronto: University of Toronto Press, 1974. 373 pages, index.
      This is the war from the Canadian point of view and is directed more toward US-Canadian relations than the war itself. The significant aspect of this work is the contention that the Canadian government, like the Russian government, did not expect the United States to make a military response in Korea. Canada, the author contends, had the job of "containing America" during this period when she seemed to be interested in swinging the big stick. See chapters one through three.

101   Yoo, Tae-Ho. <u>The Korean War, and the United Nations</u>. Belgium: University of Louvain Press, 1965.
An excellent account of the United Nations decision to enter the Korean conflict, based on French and English sources.

ARTICLES

102 Acheson, Dean "Crisis in Asia-An Examination of US Policy" <u>Department of State Bulletin</u> 22 (1950) 111-18.
Contains the 12 January 1950 speech by the Secretary of State which, historians have long claimed, so confused the issue of American defense of Korea that it invited the North Koreans to attack.

103   "Aid from U. N. to U. S. Forces Will Stay Small" <u>U.S. News and World Report</u> 29 (August 18, 1950) 24.
Military help, freely offered from members of the United Nations, represents a wide support but will in fact be limited in number.

104 Alexander, Jack. "Stormy New Boss of the Pentagon" <u>Saturday Evening Post</u> 222:5 (1949) 26-27, 67-70.
An overview of the policies of controversial Louis A. Johnson, Secretary of Defense during the early war. He made many enemies in the service.

105   "Authority of the President to Repel the Attack in Korea" <u>Department of State Bulletin</u> 23 (1950) 43-50.
Provides the legal authority for President Truman's actions, and lists the dates, places, and justification for more than 80 such previous interventions.

106   Bernstein, Barton J.   "The Week We Went to War: American Intervention in the Korean-Civil War" <u>Foreign Service Journal</u> 54 (January 1977) 6-9, 33-35. (March 1977) 8-11, 33-34.
A two part article on the United States decision to intervene. The first views Truman and Acheson attempts to determine Russian intentions, and the second focuses on the change in outlook that moved from evacuation to commitment.

107   Bradley, Omar N.   "The Path Ahead"   Army
Information Digest 5:10 (1950) 24-26.
The Chairman of the Joint Chiefs of Staff addresses
both the question of why America is involved and why
there will be a delay in getting support troops to
Korea.

108   Bradley, Omar N. "US Military Policy: 1950"
Reader's Digest 57 (October 1950) 143-154.
The Chairman of the Joint Chiefs of Staff
identifies the shift in American policy from the simple
concept of containment to contesting communism.
Stresses the need to protect Western Europe.

109 "Challenge Accepted" Time 56 (July 3, 1950) 7-8.
When the challenge of communist aggression came, it
was accepted. Truman, Johnson and Acheson took action
when the North Koreans moved beyond subversion to
conquer an independent nation.   Includes President
Truman's statement.

110   Costello, William. "Improvisation in Korea" New
Republic 123 (July 10, 1950) 13-15.
Many warned that it was too soon to turn South
Korea out on its own with the world of nations, and the
poor military showing during the invasion proved them
right.

111   Dea, Vera M.   "Justification of War"   Foreign
Policy Bulletin 31 (January 15, 1952) 5-6.
Reaffirms the communist aggression as the reason
for involvement, and sees the intervention of the United
Nations as essential for the control of the spread of
communism.

112 "Events in Korea Deepen Interest in United Nations"
Department of State Bulletin 23 (September 18, 1950)
450-451.
An address by Secretary Acheson made before the
National Citizens Committee, 7 September 1950, in which
he suggests that the United Nations action in Korea is
symbolic of all that the United Nations stands for.

113 "The Fabric of Peace" Time 56 (July 31, 1950) 10.
     President Truman, glum and ill spirited, tells the
nation of the cost of Korea. He no longer calls it a
police action, but has not yet accepted that it is in
fact a war.

114 Farley, Miriam S. "The Korean Crisis and the United
Nations" Lawrence K. Rosinger. (editor). State of Asia
New York: Alfred A. Knopf, Inc., 1951. 155-179.
     This essay, based on reports from the New York Times
and United Nations Bulletin, traces the development of
United Nations understanding and action in Korea. One
of the best statements about the why and how of the War.

115 Finletter, Thomas K. "The Meaning of Korea" Army
Information Digest 6:9 (September 1951) 3-8.
     The Secretary of the Air Force maintains the
position that the American involvement in the war came
because of the need to support the aims and ideals of
the United Nations. He writes that Korea is the point
at which the United States, and the United Nations, had
to take a stand. That the fight is about creating a
powerful defense which can be the beginning of the
efforts toward disarmament.

116 Goldman, Eric. "The President, The People, and The
Power To Make War" American Heritage 21:3 (1970) 28-35.
     Goldman makes the case that Truman acted
unconstitutionally, and unwisely, in his decision to
commit American troops in Korea, with or without United
Nations support.

117 Hoyt, Edwin P. "The United States Reaction to the
Korean Attack: A Study of the Principles of the United
Nations Charter as a Factor in American Policy-Making"
American Journal of International Law 55:1 (January
1961) 45-76.
     Hoyt defends the right of the President, as
representing a voting member of the United Nations, to
involve the United States in the Korean Conflict,
including the use of troops.

118   Ickes, Harold L. "War in Korea" <u>New Republic</u> (July 10, 1950) 17.
      Written shortly after war broke out Ickes charges that American hysteria is directly related to years of over-reaction created by McCarthyism.

119   Lawrence, David "Why Is My Son in Korea?" <u>US News</u> 30 (March 16, 1951) 64.
      Lists fourteen reasons why it is necessary for the United States to be fighting in Korea. Not realistic.

120   Matray, James I. "America's Reluctant Crusade: Truman's Commitment of Combat Troops in the Korean War" <u>Historian</u> 42 (May 1980) 437-455.
      Matray's analysis of the decision suggests that neither Truman's decision to commit troops, or his decision to do so without congressional approval, were outside the scope of normal policy. An interesting view of "the other side" of the debate.

121   Maurer, Maurer. "The Korean Conflict Was a War" <u>Military Affairs</u> 24:3 (1960) 137-145.
      Dealing with the continued United States use of the term "Police Action" the author claims that, despite the lack of congressional action, it was still a war.

122   Morris, Richard B. "The Decision to Resist the Communist Invasion of Korea" <u>Great Presidential Decisions</u>. New York: J. B. Lippincott Company, 1960.
      Text of the Truman announcement giving aid to the Korean Republic, plus commentary putting the decision into political and military context.

123 Norman, Lloyd. "Washington's War" <u>Army</u> (June 1960) 38-49.
      Claims that the United States was ill-prepared for any war, especially the one in Korea. Not only was the attack made possible because of poor intelligence by United States fact finding bodies, but the early phase of the war was nearly a disaster because of a limited understanding of the enemy, and poor supplies. Demands that the lesson of unpreparedness be learned once and for all.

124 Pelz, Stephen E.   "When the Kitchen Gets Hot, Pass the Buck: Truman and Korea in 1950" Reviews in American History 6 (December 1978) 548-555.
     Book review of volume seven Foreign Relations of the United States, 1976. Documented account of events leading to the decision. Pelz asserts that the large degree of mismanagement, particularly during the presidency of Roosevelt and Truman, was a, if not the, cause of the outbreak. Truman, Pelz contends, was too much influenced by others and did not think through his decision.

125   "President's Stand on Korea" Army Information Digest 5:8 (August 1950) 3-11.
     Extracts from the 19 July 1950 message to Congress in which President Truman justifies both his unusual decisions; involvement in the Korean War, and involvement without congressional action.

126 Smith, Beverly.   "The White House Story: Why We Went to War in Korea" Saturday Evening Post 224:19 (November 10, 1951) 22-23, 76-77, 80-88.
     This article deals with the first ten days of the Korean war, and with decision making. It appears to have had some White House support in the writing and makes, what becomes the official case for America's involvement in the war.

127 Spaatz, Carl.   "Some Answers to Korean Questions" Newsweek 36 (July 31, 1950) 17.
     This retired Air Force general answers questions about nuclear war, the F-80, the build-up of the Air Force; all questions raised by American involvement in Korea and the fears it generated.

128 Stevenson, Adlai E. "Korea in Perspective" Foreign Affairs 30:3 (1952) 349-350.
     The   then Democratic presidential candidate provides perspective on the decision to interfere, claiming that by supporting the United Nations we provided a significant move toward world security.

129 "Threats at Formosa Take Ominous Turn" Newsweek 36
(July 31, 1950) 11-13.
    While the threat of Formosa hangs in the
background, the gloomy picture from Korea is that it
might well be spring of 1951 before any serious
offensive action can be taken against the North Korean
aggression.

130 "Unflagging Use of UN Needed to Win Asian Minds"
Foreign Policy Bulletin 29 (August 11, 1950) 2-3.
    Malik's return to the United Nations brings new
charges of aggression against the United States, and
tests United Nations resolve to continue the fight in
Korea.

131 Warner, Albert L. "How the Korean Decision was
Made" Harpers 202 (June 1951) 99-106.
    Traces the decision in Washington to react with
military force to the North Korean invasion of South
Korea. Acknowledged that even if the UN had not acted
the US would have entered in.

132 "Why Are We Fighting in Korea?" U. S. Naval
Institute Proceedings 9 (1950) 1016-1017.
    Traces the chronological events leading to the
outbreak, and shows the breakdown of understanding. It
clearly puts the blame on the Russians.

The War

General Histories

BOOKS

133 Acheson, Dean G. The Korean War. New York: W. W.
Norton and Company, 1971. 153 pages, index, photographs,
maps.
    Very critical of the handling of the early phases
of the war. He expresses deep concern over MacArthur as
both military and diplomatic leader.

134   Alexander, Bevin. Korea: The First War We Lost.
New York: Hippocrene Books, 1986. 558 pages, maps.
    Bevin Alexander, Army combat historian in Korea,
has produced an excellent work. It is one of the first
to make good use of the unpublished narratives of combat
historians, and Eighth Army Corps command reports. More
than half the work is on the first year of the war.
This work attempts to show that the United States, with
the aid of the United Nations, fought two wars. One
with the North Koreans which we won, and with the
Chinese which we lost. He comes down heavily on the
costs of misunderstanding one's enemies. 1-227.

135   Appleman, Roy E. The United States Army in the
Korean War: South to the Naktong, North to the Yalu.
Washington, DC: Office of the Chief of Military History,
1961.   813 pages, index, illustrations, photographs,
maps.
    The first volume of Appleman's official histories.
Excellent detailed account, found in Chapters 1 through
12, of the pre-war contingencies, the North Korean
invasion, the battle of Taejon, counterattacks staged by
Task Force Kean, the Taejon front, the August build-up
of troops and logistics, and the final perimeter battle.

136   Berger, Carl.   The Korean Knot: A Military
Political History.   Philadelphia: University of
Pennsylvania, 1957, 1965, 1968. 255 pages, index.
    Rare history which covers the political events of
both the causes and the war itself. Excellent overview,
but limited to the political intrigue with little new
information.

137 Blair, Clay. The Forgotten War: America in Korea
1950-1953. New York: Times Books, 1987. 1136 pages,
index, maps.
    Blair is one of the few really serious historians
writing in depth about the Korean War.   This is an
excellent, well researched, and documented history.
Strong interest in the retreat and the pull-back to the
Pusan Perimeter. Strong on military leaders during the
period. Especially 3-211.

138 Bong-yon, Choy. <u>Korea: A History</u>. Tokyo: Vermont: Charles E. Tuttle Company, 1971.   475 pages, index.

This terribly biased history of the Korean War is written by a professor at the Seoul National University. He deals with the thesis that the Korean War was a revolution, and discusses both the United Nations and the American involvement in creating and supporting the revolution.   287-302.

139 Dupuy, R. Ernest. <u>The Combat History of the United States Army</u>. New York: Hawthorne Books, Inc., 1973 (2nd edition). 345 pages, index, bibliography.

A good one volume history of the organization and development of the United States army.   Chapter on the army in Korea discusses the impact of the reorganization of 1947 on the ability to field troops. Suggests the full impact of the efforts to bring about the disintegration of the army.   282-291.

140 Fehrenbach, T. R. <u>This Kind of War: A Study in Unpreparedness</u>. New York: Macmillan, 1963. 688 pages, index, photographs, maps.

One of the first really general survey histories to appear. An excellent account of the early war by a man with some first hand experience.   He stresses the fact of American unpreparedness for limited war and governmental inability to "get started."   A good study of the tension created by this political reality. Primarily compiled from post-war interviews.

141 Foot, Rosemary. <u>The Wrong War: American Policy and the Dimensions of the Korean Conflict, 1950-1953</u>. Ithaca, New York: Cornell University Press, 1985.   290 pages, index, maps, bibliography.

Foot addresses the concept of limited war and American involvement in a book which seems to document Omar Bradley's view "the wrong war, at the wrong place, and with the wrong enemy."   American efforts, from the beginning, were designed to keep China out of the war. See chapter three.

142   Goulden, Joseph C. <u>Korea: The Untold Story of the War</u>.   New York: McGraw, 1982.   690 pages, index, illustrations.

This is a good standard history which has as its advantage the author's use of the Freedom of Information Act to locate previously unexplored material.   It is well written and informative.   In discussing the early period of the war, he sides with, and is strongly supportive of MacArthur as the Allied commander.   xi - 183.

143   Hastings, Max.   <u>The Korean War</u>.   New York: Simon and Schuster, 1987.   389 pages, photographs, maps, bibliography.

Hastings, a well respected English military historian, takes a good look at the Korean War, recounting the personal experience of the individual soldiers, as well as the strategies and politics of the leadership. He covers the period of the Pusan Perimeter in detail, giving the reader the insights of both a careful historian, and an observer from the British point of view.   9-98.

144   Halliday, Jon and Bruce Cumings. <u>Korea: The Unknown War</u>. New York: Pantheon Books, 1988. 224 pages, index, illustrations, maps.

Uses interview materials from China, Russian, North and South Korea as well as the United States sources. The authors depict a war which was essentially a civil war, and which with poor response was allowed to grow into an international conflict with threats of a third World War.

145   Isserman, Maurice. <u>The Korean War</u>. America At War Series, 1992. 128 pages, index, photographs, maps, bibliography.

This volume recalls a "momentous but now largely forgotten conflict" the Korean War. This is primarily a text, written for students, but is well done and accompanied by some outstanding maps.

146   Knox, Donald. <u>The Korean War: Pusan to Chosin: An</u>
<u>Oral History</u>. Volume 1. New York: Harcourt, 1985.
     Heavily weighed toward the Marine Corps, and the
3rd Battalion, 5th Cavalry Regiment in particular, but
generally very good. Deals with the retreat (1-74), the
Pusan defense (75-126), and the breakout (126-194).

147   Lawson, Don. <u>The United States in the Korean War</u>.
New York: Abelard-Schuman, 1964. 159 pages, index, maps.
     Like so many of the general histories, this short,
simple account devotes several chapters to the retreat
and defense at Pusan. Well written and unusually fair.

148   Leckie, Robert. <u>Conflict: The History of the Korean</u>
<u>War, 1950-53</u>. New York: Putnam, 1962. 448 pages, photos.
     A controlled and competent history by a World War
II Marine who has specialized in military history.
Leckie concludes that the stalemate was, in fact, a
victory because the "Korean invasion" was repelled, and
communism suffered a major defeat.

149   Middleton, Harry J.   <u>The Compact History of the</u>
<u>Korean War</u>. New York: Hawthorn Books, Inc., 1965.   255
pages, index, maps, appendix.
     This journalist and professional documentarian has
written a readable, short, and negative history of the
Korean War. The book is wary of American ability to
fight, and the United Nations ability to lead.

150   The Ministry of National Defense, The Republic of
Korea. <u>The History of the United Nations Forces in the</u>
<u>Korean War</u>.   5 volumes. Seoul: Ministry of National
Defense, 1972-1974. Index, photographs, maps.
     A totally subjective history of the "three years'
fratricidal tragedy" designed to excuse the excesses of
the war, acknowledge the contribution of the twenty-one
nations involved in the conflict, and draw attention to
the continuing menace of the communist's view. Does
provide the South Korean point of view on the United
Nations forces, and on the military leadership of the
United Nations troops. Is an excellent source of units,
action dates, casualties. Since history is by unit, the
defense of the Pusan Perimeter is found throughout.

151 O'Ballance, Edgar. Korea, 1950-1953. Hamden,
Connecticut: Archon Books, 1969. 171 pages, index, map.
    A general history which provides an interesting
view of the decision for American involvement. The
author claims that President Truman waited to make his
decision until he had some indication from Russia that
they would not become involved on the North Korean side.
Also considers the retreat and defense of Pusan from the
view that MacArthur did not understand the Pusan
situation. 40-55, 158.

152 Rees, David. Korea: The Limited War. New York:
St. Martin's Press, 1964.   511 pages, index, maps,
appendix.
    A British author with an objective look, he
concentrates on the events leading up to the war; the
decision to stand and fight, and the early context of
the containment policy. Deals with the political as
well as the military aspects of the war.

153 Ridgway, Matthew B. The Korean War: History and
Tactics. Garden City, New York: Doubleday and Company,
1967. 268 pages, index, photographs, maps, appendix.
    While General Matthew B. Ridgway came late to
Korea this work covers the war from the beginning.
During the early phase Ridgway was doing planning, and
in a real sense was chief of staff, for Korea. His
assessment of conditions, the retreat, and the gallant
stand at Pusan are very significant.

154 Schnabel, James F. The United States Army in the
Korean War, Policy and Direction: The First Year.
Washington, DC: Office of the Chief of Military History,
1968, 1972. Index, maps, illustrations.
    This essential work, the second volume of the five
projected volumes of the United States Army and the
Korean War Series, is an excellent resource. Very
detailed, significantly footnoted, with valuable
analysis. Coverage of the retreat and the Pusan
Perimeter defense is superior. See primarily 1-125.

155 Schnabel, James F. and Robert G. Watson. <u>History of</u> <u>the Joint Chiefs of Staff: The Joint Chiefs of Staff and</u> <u>National Policy</u>.   Volume 3. Washington, DC: History Division, Part 1 - 1978, Part 2 - 1979.

Contains a significant amount of information dealing with the planning, and execution of war policy during the Korean War.   Produced in soft cover and duplicated by the Historical Division, Joint Secretariat, Joint Chiefs of Staff, it is available through Modern Military History Headquarters, National Archives.

156 Stokesbury, James L. <u>A Short History of the Korean</u> <u>War</u>. New York: Quill, William Morrow, 1988. 276 pages, index, maps.

This volume, one in a series of "Short Histories," is well done.   The tone of this work is the inevitability of our involvement in Korea once military action began.   He does a good job of reflecting the condition of the troops who, having been forced into a pocket of defense, were still able to fight.   Contains an excellent analysis of the military commanders involved.

157 Stone, Isidor F. <u>The Hidden History of the Korean</u> <u>War</u>. New York: Monthly Review Press, 1952. 364 pages, index, references.

This is still one of the more controversial works on the war.   Stone, a well known liberal journalist introduces the United States--Republic of Korea conspiracy, placing much of the blame for the war on the United States.   Excellent overview of the period in which United Nations Forces were on the withdrawal heading toward Pusan.

158 Taylor, Maxwell D. <u>The Uncertain Trumpet</u>.   New York: Harper, 1959.   203 pages.

Taylor, who was the United States Army Chief of Staff and Commander of the Eighth Army during the final period, is critical of the United States running of the Korean War, and of the early phase.

159   Thomas, Robert C. <u>The War in Korea</u>.   Aldershot, England: Gale, 1954.

While this book was written very early and without benefit of the numerous recent studies and analysis, this British officer provides a good general survey and strong support for both the United Nations involvement, and for General MacArthur's handling of the war.

160   Toland, John.   <u>In Mortal Combat: 1950 - 1953</u>. New York: William Morrow and Company, 1991.   624 pages, index, photographs, maps.

This popular historian has produced a sound history of the Korean War, and deals very well with the retreat and Pusan Perimeter.   The "Perimeter" covers an unusually large percentage of the work.   It seems to be weakened somewhat by the fact he recreates situations and dialogue where there is little historical support for his renderings.   Short anecdotes appear for little reason other than to liven up the story.   He has used both North Korean and Chinese sources and that gives it a view generally unexpected but his analysis appears overly harsh on the United States and there appear to be some key omissions.   Well written. 7-161.

161   Voorhees, Melvin B.   <u>Korean Tales</u>.   New York: Simon, 1952. 209 pages, map, chronology.

A collection of very informative essays written by the chief censor for the Eighth Army.   He had close contact with many of the military leaders and provides some interesting insight into how the early war was fought.

162   Whelan, Richard.   <u>Drawing the Line: The Korean War, 1950 - 1953</u>.   New York: Little, Brown and Company, 1990. 428 pages, index, maps, bibliography.

This work addresses "why World War III was risked to save an undemocratic republic." His answers are more descriptive than analytical, though you can tell from the title where the author comes down on the issue of involvement.   Deals with political and semi-military materials.   Pusan period covered. 100-184.

Unit Histories

BOOKS

163 Barclay, C. N. The First Commonwealth Division: The Story of British Commonwealth Land Forces in Korea, 1950-1953. Edinburgh: Thomas Nelson, 1952.
        A general history of British Forces, as well as Commonwealth units formed, during the Korean War. While the British navy was on call nearly from the beginning, the British ground forces arrived just in time to take part in the defense of the Pusan Perimeter.

164 Barth, George B. Tropic Lightning 1 Oct 1941 to 1 Oct 1966. Doralville, Georgia: Albert Love, 1967. Index, illustrations, roster.
        This unit arrived in Korea at the beginning of the war and fought throughout.   The soldiers won a Presidential Unit Citation for action 1-11 August 1950.

165 Busch, George B. Duty, The Story of the 21st Infantry Regiment. Sendai, Japan: Hyappan, 1953.
        History of the 21st Infantry from its entry into the Korean War in July of 1950, through the long retreat and the establishment of the perimeter and defense of Pusan. Continues on through the Armistice.

166 Chandler, Melbourne C. Of Garry Owen in Glory: The History of the 7th U. S. Cavalry. Annandale, Virginia: The Turnpike Press, 1960. 520 pages, index, photographs.
        Chronological account of the 7th Cavalry in Korea. Includes action in the Naktong River defense. 242-270.

167 Controvich, James T.   United States Army Unit Histories: A Reference and Bibliography. Manhattan, Kansas: Military Affairs/Aerospace Historian, 1983. Index, bibliography.
        Includes some valuable information on units which participated in the Korean War, as well as citations of ground participation, commanding generals, and an excellent bibliography.

168   Cunningham-Boothe, Ashley and Peter Farrar (editors). British Forces in the Korean War. London: The British Korean Veterans Association, 1988. 200 pages, index, illustrations.

Report on British troops who arrived late at the Pusan Perimeter. Once they were there, the British served with distinction.

169 David, Alan A. (editor). Battleground Korea: The Story of the 25th Infantry Division. Tokyo: Kyoya, 1952.

Traces division activities from the first conflict in July 1950, through the long retreat, at the Pusan Perimeter, and during the following two years. Primarily an administrative history, but very informative.

170 David, Alan A. (editor). Bayonet. Tokyo: Toppan, 1952.

A brief history of the 7th Infantry Division during the first two years of the war.

171   David, Alan A. (editor). Seventh Infantry Division, Public Information Office. Bayonet: A History of the 7th Infantry Division in Korea. Tokyo: Dai Nippon, 1953.

An administrative history of the 7th Infantry Division from its involvement in the summer of 1950 to the end of 1952.

172 Dolcater, Max W. (editor). 3rd Infantry Division in Korea. Tokyo: Toppan, 1953. Pictures, maps, awards, casualties.

An extensive look at the 3rd Infantry Division through the Korean war. Lists activities, battles, awards, and those killed in action.

173 Eighth US Army, Military History Section. The First Ten Years: A Short History of the Eighth United States Army 1944-1954. Tokyo: Army AG Administrative Center, 1954.

This fairly light account of the Eighth Army, focuses on administrative rather than combat coverage, but is informative, particularly about TO & E.

174 Farner, F. (editor). The First Team. Atlanta: Love, 1952.

Primarily a yearbook of the United States 1st Cavalry Division in Korea, with descriptive unit histories from 18 July 1950 to January 1952, but it covers the Pusan period.

175 Grey, Jeffrey. The Commonwealth Armies and the Korean War. New York: St. Martin's Press, 1988. 244 pages, index, bibliography.

Relates British efforts in Korea, but sees them as less interested in Korea, and more an effort to improve relations with the United States, and to identify itself as a partner in the United Nations.

176 Jacobs, Bruce. Soldiers; the Fighting Divisions of the Regular Army. New York: Norton, 1958. 367 pages, photographs.

Brief history of the twenty one divisions of the regular army, with considerations of 2nd, 7th, 24th, 25th, 43rd infantry and the 1st cavalry which were involved in Korea, several in the retreat and defense at Pusan.

177 The Legacy of Custer's 7th U. S. Cavalry in Korea. Paducah, Kentucky: Turner Publishing Company, 1990. 128 pages, index, photographs.

The 7th Cavalry arrived in Korea in July of 1950 and were immediately put into combat. This unit history does a good job covering the division activities during the retreat and Pusan defense. Chapters one - five.

178 Linklater, Eric. Our Men in Korea. London: Her Majesty's Stationery Office, 1952.

Accounts of the 27th Brigade, British, which consisted of the 1st Battalion of the Middlesex Regiment and the 1st Battalion of the Argyll and Sutherland Highlanders Regiment, the 45th Field Artillery Regiment, Royal Artillery. A battalion of Australian volunteers was added during the summer of 1950. These troops saw action along Congchon.

179 MacDonald, Callum A. <u>Britain and the Korean War</u>. Oxford: Basil Blackwell, Ltd., 1990. 112 pages, index, map.

Great Britain, the author says, went to war in 1950 to consolidate the Anglo-American alliance and to resist communist aggression goals. The decision owed nothing to any direct importance of Korea to Britain. The Commonwealth troops fought in, but not for, Korea. The involvement of British troops in the Pusan defense (August 1950) was more linked to commitments in Europe than military needs in Korea.

180 Malcolm, George I. <u>The Argylls in Korea</u>. London, Nelson, 1952.

A brief account of the Argyll and Sutherland, holders of a great military tradition, thrown into the fighting in 1950 more as a token than a military unit. The formal outfit went on to make a significant contribution.

181 Moore, Clark C. <u>U. S. 1st Cavalry Division: The Second United States Infantry Division in Korea 1951</u>. Tokyo: Toppan Printing Company, 1951, reprint 1992. 227 pages, maps.

A yearbook presentation of the military, social and personnel activities of the 1st Cavalry Division in the first year of the war. Has all the problems of a service book, but does provide a good bit of information about the division.

182 O'Neill, Robert. <u>Australia in the Korean War</u>. Volume One. Canberra, Australia: The Australian War Memorial and Australian Government Publishing Service, 1981.

Deals with the commitment of Australian naval, air, and ground troops, June 1950 - July 1950. 1-77.

183 Stadtmauer, Saul. (editor). <u>24th Forward, A Pictorial History of the Victory Division in Korea</u>. Tokyo: Toppan Press, 1953.

An account, with excellent pictures, of the 24th Infantry Division throughout Korea. The 24th was heavily involved in the defense of the Pusan Perimeter.

184   United States Army, 1st Cavalry Division.   The First Cavalry Division in Korea 18 July 1950 - 18 January 1952.   Atlanta: Love, 1957.

A history of the 1st Cavalry Division from its commitment in the first weeks of the war, to its return to Japan in 1951.   The 1st Cavalry was involved in the defense of Pusan.

185   United States Military Academy, Department of Military Art and Engineering. Operations in Korea. West Point, New York: United States Military Academy, 1956.

A brief, but fairly inclusive, account of American military units in Korea, including operational movement during the Pusan Perimeter defense.

ARTICLES

186   "Roll Call: The Outfits Ticketed for the Korean Job" Newsweek 36 (July 31, 1950) 13.

The six major combat divisions to fight in Korea are described in capsule profile: 1st Cavalry, 1st Marines, 2nd Infantry, 7th Infantry, 24th Infantry, 25th Infantry.

187   "Canada's Army in Korea" Canadian Army Journal 9 (1955) (1) 5-29, (2) 20-42, (3) 20-42, (4) 16-34, (5) 21-34.

A five part history of the Canadian involvement, part one dealing with the Pusan Perimeter period, when three destroyers joined forced on 30 June 1950. Contains a brief bibliography of Canadian and communist forces.

188   Geer, Andrew. "Eight Perilous Hours Inside Red Lines" Saturday Evening Post 224 (1951) 26-27, 92-96.

An account of the 41st British Independent Commandoes, who entered the war shortly after hostilities, and took part in a raid 150 miles behind the lines.   Great Britain was an aggressive partner during the early days of the war.

Autobiographies, Biographies, and Memoirs

BOOKS

189   Dean, William F. and William L. Worden. <u>General Dean's Story</u>. New York: Viking Press, 1954. 305 pages, photographs.

General Dean was captured during the early months of the Korean War and held captive until the end of the war. His accounts of the early confusion during the first communist drive are lively, entertaining, frustrating, and a frightening reminder of just how under-prepared America was for a war of any kind.

190 MacArthur, Douglas. <u>Reminiscences</u>. New York: Da Capo Paperback, 1964. 448 pages, index.

Surprisingly poor accounting of a life of military service. Part nine of this memoir deals with Korea. Talks about the use of troops and the problems of press censorship. 325-350.

191 Oliver, Robert T. <u>Syngman Rhee: The Man Behind the Myth</u>. New York: Dodd Mead and Company, 1954.   380 pages, index, appendix.

This biography, written by a man who knew and worked with Rhee, is a very sensitive account of the turbulent years of his life, and deals in considerable depth with the years identified as the war for Korean independence.

192   Schaller, Michael. <u>Douglas MacArthur: The Far Eastern General</u>. New York: Oxford University Press, 1989. 320 pages, index, maps.

A far from flattering account of Douglas MacArthur as the supreme military commander in the Far East. Schaller includes a look at MacArthur's view of his commanders. Of particular interest is his comment on General Walker who he felt had lost the fighting edge.

193   Smith, Robert.   <u>MacArthur in Korea: The Naked Emperor</u>. New York: Simon & Schuster, 1982. 256 pages, index, photographs, maps, bibliography.

      In this assessment of MacArthur's role in Korea, Smith is willing to admit to MacArthur's skills as an advocate of action, as well as a very courageous soldier, but stops there. He sees MacArthur as a demigod whose own inability to listen and take criticism pushed him into a position that was politically misinformed and militarily outdated. MacArthur did not understand the Pusan defense.

194   Suh, Dae-Sook.   <u>Kim Il Sung: The North Korean Leader</u>. New York: Columbia University Press, 1988. 441 pages, index, photographs.

      This North Korean leader held power longer than most heads of government, and was a central power in international affairs. This work shows his strength and weakness, deals with accomplishments during the war. See chapter seven.

195   Sun Yup, Paik.   <u>From Pusan to Panmunjom</u>. Washington: Brassey's (US), Inc. 1992. 269 pages, illustrations.

      When North Korea invaded the South, Colonel Paik Sun Yup was commanding the 1st ROK division. He rose in the rank to become Korea's first four-star general and was South Korea's representative at the peace talks. He delivers a vital first hand account of the early defeats, Pusan and the perimeter, and the eventual breakout. Very supportive forewords by General Matthew Ridgway and General James Van Fleet, and pages 1 - 48.

196 Truman, Harry S. <u>Memoirs, Volume 2, Years of Trial and Hope</u>. Garden City, New York: Doubleday and Company, 1956.

      President Truman was in the middle of the conflict both in and about Korea. As Commander-in-Chief his approval was necessary for almost any policy change. His early involvement is well documented, and indexed.

ARTICLES

197 Hillman, R. L. "End of a Leader" Army 13:8 (March, 1963) 25-29.
     The death of Lt. Collins (presumably a fictional characterization of a platoon gunnery officer) designed to show the initiative of command at all phases of leadership. Set during the early phases of the war.

198 "Kim Il Sung" Army Digest 24:10 (1969) 32.
     A short but informative account of the life of the North Korean leader from his birth in 1912 until 1965. It suggests that Kim was all powerful in his varied roles as Premier, General Secretary of both the Central Committee and the Korean Labor Party, and as the Supreme Commander of the Armed Forces.

199 Parrott, L. "And Now MacArthur of Korea" New York Times Magazine (August 20, 1950) 50-51.
     Identifies MacArthur, now 70, as a powerful and hardworking leader who may well be the salvation of the United States in Asia.

Soldiers in Action

BOOKS

200 Lord, Lewis. The Medal of Honor. No publisher, date.
     Two Korean War heroes, John Page and Charles Loring are honored in this account of the early war.

201 Marshall, Samuel L. A. Infantry Operations and Weapons Usage in Korea (Winter 1950-51). London: Greenhill Books, 1988. (first edition Boston: Johns Hopkins University, 1953). 147 pages, illustrations, notes.
     Discusses the operations of Eighth Army during the winter of 1950 by looking at the behavior of men, the use of weapons and the nature of the infantry tactics. Not very complimentary of any of the areas discussed.

202   Mesko, Jim.   <u>Armor in Korea</u>.   Squad Sig
Publications, 1983.   80 pages, photographs.
    Illustration of armor at the Pusan Perimeter,
considerable detailed drawings and discussion of early
availability and use.

203 Murphy, Edward F. <u>Korean War Heroes</u>.   Novato,
California: Presidio Press, 1992. 304 pages, index, map,
bibliography.
    This interesting account of Medal of Honor winners
during the Korean Conflict includes two chapters dealing
with those medals awarded during the Pusan defense.

                        ARTICLES

204 Barth, George B. "The First Days in Korea" <u>Combat
Forces Journal</u> 2:8 (March 1952) 21-24.
    The overconfidence suffered by so many of the
United States troops when they first entered Korea was
quickly replaced by stubborn determination.

205   Blair, William D. Jr. "Journey Beyond Fear"
<u>Reader's Digest</u> 59 (1951) 1-4.
    Blair, a war correspondent, was present during the
September 1950 battle for Seoul. He was wounded. This
provides a sensitive account of the fear, pain, and
anxiety of combat.

206 Davidson, B. "Why Half Our Combat Soldiers Fail to
Shoot" <u>Collier's</u> 130 (November 8, 1952) 16-18.
    Based on an interview with S. L. A. Marshall who
says failure of aggression on the battlefield can be
traced to early training. During World War II there
were cases where only 37 men out of 1000 fired their
weapons. During the Korean War it was about one out of
two.

207   Hershey, Lewis B. "Mobilization of Manpower"
<u>Quartermaster Review</u> 30 (1950) 4-5, 144-147.
    The Director of Selective Service explains the
problems in raising a three-million man force from
veterans, reservists, and new recruits.

208 Martin, Harold H. "How Do Our Negro Troops Measure Up?" Saturday Evening Post 23 (June 16, 1951) 30-31. Illustrated.

The combat record of the black 24th Infantry Regiment was not all that good. But when integrated into other units black troops served with distinction. Argues that segregation in the military must end.

209 Parks, Floy L. "Defense Begins at Home" Army Information Digest 8:1 (1953) 7-12.

The author proposes that it was the lack of adequate peace-time preparation that is to blame for the bad showing of United States troops.

Task Force Smith

ARTICLES

210 Balmforth, Edward E. "Getting Our ROKS Off" Combat Forces Journal 1 (1951) 22-25.

Describes the effect of the August 1950 encounter when a thousand ROK soldiers were integrated into the United States 17th Infantry (7th Division) as replacements. The experiment was not well planned and caused considerable difficulties.

211 Cannon, Michael. "Task Force Smith: A Study in (un)Preparedness and (ir)Responsibility" Military Review 68:2 (February 1988) 63-74.

Task Force Smith was the first American unit in combat. They suffered heavy losses due to the outdated nature of their equipment, the poor quality of ammo, and the unrealistic nature of their peace-time training.

212 Colon, William. "Task Force Smith" Infantry 70 (January - February, 1980) 35-37, illustrations, maps.

Short account of the formation of, deployment, and cost of the first American unit to face the North Koreans.

213   Flint, Roy K.   "Task Force Smith and the 24th Division: Delay and Withdrawal, 5-19 July, 1950" Charles E. Heller and William A. Stofft. (editors). America's First Battles, 1776 - 1965. Lawrence, Kansas: University Press of Kansas, 1986.   266-299.
    A detailed account of the first battle, but more than that, a seasoned account of military unpreparedness and uncoordinated action.   An important and brave sacrifice, but for what?

214   High, Gil. "Never Again" Soldiers 45:9 (September 1990) 24-25.
    Discusses the failures imposed on Task Force Smith, and yet acknowledges the significance of this force.

215   Ickes, Harold L. "Once More We Fight For Time" New Republic 123 (July 31, 1950) 17.
    The United States has been pushed into a beachhead with no place else to go, trading men for time while the "corrupt police state of South Korea" crumbles.

216 Maddox, Robert. "War in Korea: The Desperate Times" American History Illustrated 13:4 (1978) 26-38.
    Describes the initial actions in July of 1950, primarily the role of "Task Force Smith" (which suffered 50% casualties), and the 24th Division which, short of weapons and ammunition, suffered great losses of men and real estate.

Survival and Retreat

BOOKS

217   Bussey, Charles.   Firefight at Yechon. New York: Brassey's (US), Inc., 1991. 265 pages, appendix, photographs, maps.
    The author, an officer of the 77th Engineers (Combat), was a member of the black outfit which fought at the battle of Yechon. He is very supportive of the black as a fighting man -- though favoring the integration of troops that was taking place -- and critical of Appleman's reporting of the inefficiency of black troops.

218   Gugeler, Russell A.   <u>Combat Actions in Korea:</u>
<u>Infantry, Artillery, and Armor</u>. Washington, DC: Combat
Forces Press Institute, 1954. Reprint 1970. 260 pages,
maps.

Contains numerous battle narratives of the early
days, compiled by official army historians from action
reports.   Original manuscripts, longer and more
detailed, are available for study at the Army's Center
of Military History, Washington, DC.

219   Hopkins, William B. <u>One Bugle: No Drum</u>.   Chapel
Hill: Algonquin Books of Chapel Hill, 1986. 274 pages,
bibliography, appendix.

Chapter two, "Retreat to Pusan" is an excellent
account of elements of the 1st Marines and Eighth Army
during the initial retreat, and the defense perimeter.
The remainder follows through the retreat from Chosin.

220   Noble, Harold Joyce.   <u>Embassy at War</u>.   Seattle:
University of Washington Press, 1975. 328 pages, index,
map.

Harold Noble was an expert on Korean affairs, and
First Secretary of the American Embassy at the time of
the North Korean invasion. He recounts the period from
25 June 1950 to 29 September 1950 during which the
Americans, as well as the Republic of Korea, suffered
defeat, retreated, finally taking a stand at Pusan, and
then breaking out. His background and insights paint an
interesting picture of the early days.

221   Riley, John W. Jr. and Wilbur Schramm.   <u>The Reds</u>
<u>Take A City: The Communist Occupation of Seoul</u>.   New
Brunswick, New Jersey: Rutger University Press, 1951.
210 pages, index.

A somewhat dramatic eyewitness account of the North
Korean occupancy of the capital on 28 June 1950. While
early accounts discuss the failed efforts at defense and
the defeat of the city, most of the work, however, is
spent dealing with questions of survival in Seoul.

ARTICLES

222   Berbert, Henry.   "Engineer Field Notes -- Korea:
Delaying the Advance in the First Few Days" Military
Engineer 42 (1950) 433-434.

The role of the ROK engineers, guided by American
advisors, during the retreat 30 June - 5 July 1950 when
destruction of key bridges and cratering roads was about
all that could be done to slow the enemy. The other side
of the argument is that the premature blowing of key
bridges had cut off or destroyed hundreds of ROK troops.

223   Bell, James A.   "The Brave Men of No Name Ridge"
Life 29:9 (1950) 34. Also in Great Readings from Life.
729-32.

An account of United States troops at the first
battle of Naktong in August of 1950.

224   Denson, John.   "What Hurt Was to See Us Retreat"
Colliers 126:10 (1950) 17, 58.

This is a description of the first contacts of
United States forces with the North Korean Army, and of
Sgt. Leonard Smith, one of the first Marines to be
wounded. Expresses considerable shock over the retreat
of Americans.

225   Duncan, David. "The First Five Days" Life 29:2
(1950) 20-27.

Duncan, a photographer for Life was one of the
first photo-journalists in Korea. His words and photos
narrate events from the evacuation of American citizens
to the first visit from MacArthur.

226   Falls, Cyril. "A Window on the World: Still
Delaying-actions in Korea" The Illustrated London News
217 (July 29, 1950) 172.

General MacArthur was defeated at the battle of Kum
River, the line where he assumed he could finally stop
the North Koreans. Now he must retreat into a defense
perimeter, and fight for time.

227   Higgins, Marguerite.   "Terrible Days in Korea"
Saturday Evening Post 223 (August 19, 1950) 26-27.
        Account of the war's most famous female
correspondent who accompanied troops on the Seoul to
Taejon retreat. A well written folksy approach which
makes no effort to hide her opinions which are,
generally, unfavorable.

228 "Indo-China Next on Kremlin's List?" Newsweek 36
(August 14, 1950) 15-19.
        In battles along the Naktong River line the United
States meets the communist who are desperate. Evidence
grows that the Chinese are training and equipping Viet
Minh troops for an expanded war. The question is, can
they stop the war in Korea?

229 "In the Cause of Peace" Time 56 (July 10, 1950) 7-
11.
        Announces the Command of General "Bulldog" Walker
as the combat zone continues to shrink in size forming
a perimeter around Pusan. General Walker issues his
order to hold the line at all costs.

230   Lantham, Henry J. "I Saw Us Almost Get Licked in
Korea" Saturday Evening Post 223:18 (1950) 28-29, 131-
133.
        A congressman's view after a short visit to
Korea.   Greatly disheartened by the suffering and
defeat, he nevertheless concludes that, given the
American state of unpreparedness, the troops are doing
very well in the fight.

231 Marshall, S. L. A. "Our Army in Korea: The Best
Yet" Harper's 203 (1951) 21-27.
        A most favorable account of the first year of the
Eighth Army in Korea. Marshall, a first class military
historian, gives an eye-witness account of the best of
the Eighth Army. Repeated in Combat Forces Journal and
Detroit News. This is a very good look at what faced
United States troops during the early fighting.

232   Marshall, S. L. A. "This is the War in Korea"
Combat Forces Journal 1:11 (June 1951) 15-22.
      This distinguished American historian takes a long
hard look at the first few months of the war. While he
finds that many mistakes were made, and troops and
equipment limited, the Eighth Army was hard and tough
and were fighting a good fight.

233   Martin, Harold H. "The Colonel Saved the Day"
Saturday Evening Post 223:11 (1950) 32-33, 187, 189-190.
      Lt. Colonel John Michaelis, 27th Infantry Regiment
Commander, held his assigned defense position in the
face of heavy North Korean infantry action near
Chindong-ni.

234   Nicholson, Dennis D. "Creeping Tactics"   Marine
Corps Gazette 42 (1958) 20-26.
      Describes the tactics of the first few months of
the war as North Koreans crept into American positions
and launched devastating attacks from all directions.

235   Paschall, Rod. "Special Operations in Korea"
Conflict 7:2 (1987) 155-178.
      One of the few items to discuss North Korean
partisans who, during the early months, inflicted nearly
70,000 casualties among the North Korean troops. The
United Nations did not make the most of these partisans
because they were basically disorganized, and because
there was no role for them in the negotiations.

236 Williams, John H. "Stand or Die" Army 35:8 (August
1985) 56-68, photos.
      Deals with the fighting during the early phase of
the war, and at the Pusan Perimeter. North Korean
commanders had been ordered to conquer all of South
Korea by 15 August 1950 and they were running out of
time. The United Nations troops were running out of
space. By early August the fighting had become
desperate and troops were aware that there was no where
else to run.

The Pusan Perimeter

BOOKS

237 Hinshaw, Arned L. Heartbreak Ridge: Korea, 1951.
New York: Praeger, 1951. 146 pages, index.
    Excellent book on the beginning of the static war.
Two early chapters deal with the outbreak of the war,
and Pusan defense.

238   Hoyt, Edwin P. America's Wars & Military
Excursions. New York: McGraw-Hill Publishing Company,
1987. 539 pages, index, maps, bibliography.
    A brief, and very general account, of the early days
of the Korean War, including some discussion of the
defense of the Pusan Perimeter. 424-434.

239 Hoyt, Edwin P. The Pusan Perimeter: Korea, 1950.
New York: Stein and Day Publishers, 1984. 310 pages,
index, photographs, bibliography.
    The only full length study of the Pusan Perimeter
which concentrates on the amazing defense that was
conducted there. This narrative, told by a popular and
respectable historian, follows from the invasion,
through the first efforts to delay the North Koreans,
the retreat to Naktong, the formation of the first and
second defense line for the Perimeter, and the many
efforts to break the United Nations defense. Contains
a limited bibliography.

ARTICLES

240 De Reus, C. C. "The Perimeter Pays Off" Combat
Forces Journal 3:5 (1952) 31-34.
    Excellent account of patrol action while serving
with the 3rd Battalion, 7th Regiment, 3rd Infantry
Division, during the perimeter period.

241   Jaeger, Vernon. "Experiences in Korea" <u>Military Chaplain</u> (October 1950) 1-2.
      A United States Army chaplain serving on the line makes some observations on what took place during the first few months of the war. He was astonished at the poor preparation and support of the troops thrown into battle.

242   Kleinman, Forrest K.   "The Tactician of Danger Forward" <u>Army</u> 9 (November 1958) 26-29.
      Short supportive article which acknowledged General John Church of the 24th Division, as a major tactician in this bewildering period of the Korean War.

243   "Korea: Test of Strength" 1:1 <u>Combat Forces Journal</u> (August 1950) 38-39.
      South Korea was outmatched and outsmarted right from the beginning, and could not hold Korea. The test was if the United States was able to hold the North Korean Army long enough for men and supplies to arrive in time to aid the South.

244   Lawrence, W. H. "A Day in the Life of a Platoon" <u>New York Times Magazine</u> (September 10, 1950) 13-14.
      An accounting in story form of life among the troops while holding the Pusan Perimeter line. Lawrence identifies life on the line as long hours of waiting, and short periods of combat.

245   "New Troops Bolster Battered GI's" <u>Newsweek</u> 36 (August 7, 1950) 15-17.
      As North Korea continues to attack, seeking to break the Pusan Perimeter and drive the United Nations forces into the sea, a steady stream of newly formed army and marine units land troops and prepare to join the battle for Pusan.

246   Russell, George H. "Defense On An Extended Front" <u>Infantry School Quarterly</u> 43:2 (1953) 60-64.
      The 23rd Infantry Regiment defended a 16,000 yard front on the Taegu-Pusan Perimeter during August and September of 1950, and did it successfully. This article tries to explain how it was possible.

247   Tate, James H. "The First Five Months" Army Information Digest 6:3 (March 1951) 40-48.
This is the first of a long series on the fighting of the war, and covers the details of the battle fought by United Nations troops from the initial invasion to the perimeter at Pusan.

248   "War in Asia" Time 56 (July 17, 1950) 17-18.
Failure after failure forces United States troops into a ever tightening perimeter of last defense about the port of Pusan. Discusses weapons available for the defense of the perimeter.

249   "War in Asia" Time 56 (July 24, 1950) 20-21.
The communist drive threatens to cut the rail line, to encircle and destroy the forces of the United States on their first line of defense at the Pusan Perimeter.

250   "War in Asia" Time 56 (July 31, 1950) 15-17.
While the United States troops steadily retreat toward the build-up area around Pusan, there is no reason to believe that the communists are not planning to expand the war into Indo-China.

251   "War in Asia" Time 56 (August 7, 1950) 18-20.
General Walker issues a "stand-or-die" order as the United Nations moves into a hastily created perimeter of defense around Pusan. MacArthur estimates 90,000 North Korean troops ready to attack.

252   "War in Asia" Time 56 (August 21, 1950) 18-22.
The withdrawals have halted as the United States beachhead holds. The minimum perimeter holds as the line of the outer perimeter counterattacks against North Korean forces.

253   "War in Asia" Time 56 (August 28, 1950) 21-23.
Discusses the choice faced by United Nations forces, to attack or move back into a defense perimeter. The decision to move into a perimeter definitely saved the situation.

254 "War in Asia" <u>Time</u> 56 (September 4, 1950) 20.
    The perimeter defense is holding as United Nations forces continue to gather men and supplies. Command is now voicing concern about over-confidence. This seems to be the extreme of "morale-building" articles.

255 Wood, Lt. Col. "Artillery Support For The Brigade In Korea" <u>Marine Corps Gazette</u> (June 1951) 16-23.
    Very interesting account of an artillery commander who set up the first marine artillery support for the brigade when it landed during August of 1950 in defense of the Pusan Perimeter.

256 Worden, William L. "Britain's Gallantry is Not Dead" <u>Saturday Evening Post</u> 223 (1951) 28-29, 94-96.
    The 27th British Brigade fought effectively against North Korean troops advancing in August against the Perimeter.

Attack and Counterattack

ARTICLES

257 Appleman, Roy E. "At the Bowling Alley" <u>Time</u> 56 (September 4, 1950) 21-22.
    The 27th Infantry Regiment 25th Division under Colonel Mike Michaeus met the North Korean "Eighth Route Army" near Taegu in a battle which the defense lost.

258 Appleman, Roy E. "The Bowling Alley Fight" <u>Army</u> 11:9 (April 1961) 44-49.
    An account of the Wolfhounds, 27th Infantry Regiment, 25th Infantry Division, who held during seven days of North Korean infantry and armor attack near the village of Sio-ri.

259 Edwards, James. "Action at Tongmyongwon" <u>Infantry School Quarterly</u> 38:1 (1951) 66-83.
    The 2nd Battalion, 23rd Infantry, 2nd Division held the enemy from 21-24 August 1950, thus avoiding a bridgehead across the Naktong River.

260   Edwards, James. "Naktong Defense" Infantry School Quarterly 38:2 (1951) 77-92.
    Account of the 2nd Battalion, 23rd Infantry, 2nd Division which held 18,000 yards of front, and partially destroyed two North Korean Divisions from 31 August to 16 September 1950, who tried to attack.

261   Glasgow, William M. Jr.   "Korean Ku Klux Klan" Combat Forces Journal 2:7 (1952) 18-24.
    More than 2000 torch-carrying North Koreans attack the 2nd platoon, Company B, 23rd Infantry, 2nd Division cutting them off. Many of the men moved back through enemy lines to their own areas.

262   Gugeler, Russell A. "Attack Along a Ridgeline" Combat Forces Journal 4:10 (May 1954) 22-27.
    Naktong River, 15 August 1950, 2nd platoon, Company A, 1st Battalion of the 34th Infantry Regiment conducted a disastrous attack, which led to the death of over half the members. Gugeler describes the role of the 34th infantry, fighting along the ridge after a break in the central section of the Pusan Perimeter near the Naktong River on 6 August 1950, where a hard driving North Korean force was stopped.

263   Gugeler, Russell A. "The Defense of a Battery Position" Combat Forces Journal 4:11 (June 1954) 34-37.
    Discusses the defense tactics and defense of a firing battery position when Battery A, 64th Field Artillery Battalion in support of the 34th Infantry was attacked during September 1950.   The gunners became grunts and saved the position and their guns.

264   Robinson, William G.   "Counterattack on the Naktong, 1950" Leavenworth Papers No. 13.   United States Army Command and Staff Colleges: Leavenworth, Kansas: December, 1985.   1-38.
    Sets the stage for the Pusan Perimeter and for counterattacks along the "bulge line" as North Korean forces push the last desperate attacks.

Breakout

BOOKS

265   Heinl, Robert D. Jr. <u>Victory at High Tide: The Inchon-Seoul Campaign</u>.   New York: J. B. Lippincott, 1968.   315 pages, index, photographs, maps.

MacArthur was not convinced that the landing at Inchon would be sufficient for the Eighth Army to break out of Pusan and move north.   He felt that General Walker and the defenders of Pusan had been retreating so long they might be unable to take the offensive even if the Inchon attack was successful.   Therefore, MacArthur suggested other possible landings (147-48) to break the hold, the replacement of Walker as Army Commander (246-248) as well as lack of confidence in Eighth Army in general (246-256).   Events were to prove him wrong.

266   Higgins, Marguerite. <u>War in Korea</u>.   Garden City, New York: Doubleday, 1951.   221 pages, photographs, maps.

Many military leaders, including MacArthur, considered Marguerite Higgins to be a pain.   However she was the first female, and one of the first correspondents, to arrive where the action was.   Her book covered the first few weeks of the war, moving slightly beyond the breakout from Pusan, during which she became very discouraged about the ability of the American forces to hold.   She makes lively comments about General Dean and General Walker, the state of the troops, the nature of the enemy and allies, and discusses the effect of a proposed loss in Korea.

ARTICLE

267   Quinn, Joseph M. "Catching the Enemy Off Guard" <u>Armor</u> 60:4 (1951) 46-48.

Describes the 89th Tank Battalion (Task Force Dolvin) which led the breakout of the Pusan Perimeter in September 1950.

Naval Support at the Perimeter

BOOKS

268   Cagle, Malcolm W. and Frank A. Manson.   The Sea War. Annapolis: United States Naval Institute, 1957. 554 pages, index, photographs, maps.
Chapters one and two are helpful in understanding use of naval gun fire to interdict along coastal targets.   Coastal fire was also used during the defense of Pusan.   It deals with an aspect of the war that is poorly understood.

269   Field, James A., Jr.   History of United States Naval Operations: Korea.   Washington, DC: Government Printing Office, 1962. 499 pages, index, photographs, maps.
Certainly the best single volume history of a significant, but primarily unknown aspect of the Korean War.   Naval coverage of the coastal lanes, bombardment of select targets, and a major share of the air war are covered for the Pusan Perimeter period.   Of great significance was the naval support of Pusan in terms of reinforcements and supplies.

270   Hallion, Richard P.   The Naval Air War in Korea. Baltimore: The Nautical and Aviation Publishing Company of America, 1986.   244 pages, index, photographs, maps.
Chapter one, "Preserving the Pocket," traces naval air support for the first Anglo-American air strike 4 July 1950 - from the USS Triumph - to the terrible toll taken during the Naktong River fighting.

271 Howarth, Stephen.   To Shining Sea: A History of the United States Navy, 1775-1991.   New York: Random House, 1991.   620 pages, index, bibliography.
Excellent history of the United States Navy, showing the growth of naval resources and tactics. Chapter 18 gives a good overview of the Korean War, including a discussion of early work at Pusan.

272 Hoyt, Edwin P. Carrier Wars. New York: McGraw-Hill Publishing, 1989. 274 pages, index, bibliography.

A very brief but informative account of the role played by the navy task force in the initial fighting, and defense of the Pusan Perimeter. 232 -241.

273   Korean Cruise USS St. Paul CA 73.   Berkeley, California: Lederer, 1951.

The account of the USS St. Paul, one of the first heavy cruisers to arrive in Korean waters, 12 August 1950, in support of ground troops. It continued on station until 21 May 1951.

274   The Korean Cruise of the USS Tingey DD 539. San Diego, California: Davidson, 1951.

Narrative of the contribution made by an American destroyer in the early days of the Korean War. These "greyhounds of the sea" provided bombardments, escort, and supply missions.

275 Miller, Max. I'm Sure We've Met Before. New York: E. P. Dutton & Company, 1951. 191 pages, photographs, index.

An interesting and first hand account of the navy's role in the early days of the Korean War. In command of men who thought they were heading home for a long peace, Lt. Commander Miller recounts the difficulties while the navy provided firepower, and supplies, during the dark days, and the eventual breakout.

276 Schratz, Paul R. Submarine Commander. Louisville: University of Kentucky Press, 1988. 322 pages, index.

Chapter nine and ten of this work by one of the United States navy's most innovative submarine commanders, deals with the transition from World War II service to special duty aboard the USS Pickerel during the Korean War. Some excellent information about the use of the submarine in this primarily land war.

277 Smith, M. S. The Korea Cruise USS Philippine Sea CV-47. Berkeley, California: Lederer, 1951.

From July 1950 to June 1951 the USS Philippine Sea operated off the coast giving aid to the Perimeter.

ARTICLES

278   Denson, John. "Captain Thach's Phantom Carrier" Collier's 126 (1950) 18-19, 52-56.
       Describes the operations of the escort carrier USS Sicily and its destroyer escort, while operating off the coast of Korea during the first two months of the war. The USS Sicily provided air support and cover.

279 Fleming, Kenneth. "Hell Run Over Korea" Leatherneck 33 (1950) 18-20.
       Discusses the difficulty for carrier-based air photographers who risked life and limb to eventually provide clear pictures of the Pusan Perimeter thus making the defense possible.

280 Griffin, Harry L. "The Navy in Korean Waters" Army Information Digest 6:12 (December 1951) 12-22.
       Points out that the navy was involved in the war from the very beginning, offering support both in terms of firepower on selected targets, and logistical support to the ground troops.

281   Holly, D. C. "The ROK Navy: Reorganization After World War II with US Aid; Its Record During the Korean Conflict" U. S. Naval Institute Proceedings 78 (November 1952) 1218-1225.
       Two United States destroyers were recommissioned in the ROK navy, the first in 375 years, as the United States developed a naval force for South Korea. Begun at the time of the Pusan Perimeter, and of some use then.

Air Power at the Perimeter

BOOKS

282 Cleveland, W. M. Mosquitos in Korea. Portsmouth: Peter E. Randall Publisher, 1991.   312 pages, index.
       Published by the Mosquito Association, it provides an interesting and detailed account of the daily operations in defense of the perimeter.   Scattered throughout but is indexed.

283 Futrell, Robert F. The United States Air Force in
Korea, 1950 -1953. New York: Duell, Sloan and Pearce,
1961. Revised edition 1983. 774 pages, illustrations,
photographs, maps, notes.
   Considers the air war in Korea not so much as the
Korean experience, but as an example of what not to do
next time. Chapters one to four recount the immediate
reaction to the outbreak of war, preparation and
eventual defense of the Pusan Perimeter. Futrell, of the
Air University, deals with the transition between more
conventional warfare and jets. A good and factual
history of the recreation of the Far East Air Force and
its "decisive role" in the Korean War.

284   Futrell, Robert F. United States Air Force
Operations in the Korean Conflict, 25 June - 1 November
1950. United States Air Force Historical Division,
Historical Study, No. 71, 1952.
   This department of the Air Force book is a
restricted but introductory account of the role of the
United States Air Force, from the day of America's
involvement to the end of this period. Limited but good
coverage.

285   Goldberg, Alfred. (editor). A History of the
United States Air Force, 1907-1957. Princeton: D. Van
Nostrand Co., 1957. 277 pages, index, photographs.
   Chapter 24 provides a clear and concise account of
air action during the prolonged defense of the Pusan
Perimeter.

286 Jackson, Robert. Air War Over Korea. New York:
Scribners, 1973. 175 pages, photographs, maps, appendix,
bibliography.
   A good initial history of the role of air power
during the Korean War. The first three chapters deal
with close air support in defense of evacuations,
covering the retreat south, and defense of the troops
during the Pusan Perimeter. Also discusses the bombing
efforts against North Korea which were designed to limit
supplies to the besieging forces.

287 Stewart, James T. Airpower: The Decisive Force in
Korea.   Princeton: D. Van Nostrand Co., 1957.   310
pages, illustrations.
     Holds that airpower played the decisive role in
the fighting in Korea.   While he presents his case
fairly well, he makes some questionable claims about the
value of airpower during the early retreat.   Various
chapters in this book were published originally as
articles in the Air University Quarterly Review.

ARTICLES

288 "The Air-Ground Operation in Korea" Air Force 34
(1951) 19-58.
     The main part of this issue is devoted to a lengthy
consideration of the role played by the Air Force in
flying ground support missions during the first six
months of the war.

289 Clark, Mark W. "What Kind of Air Support Does the
Army Want? An Interview with General Mark W. Clark"
Air Force 33 (1950) 24-25, 52.
     Discusses the need for close support between army
and air cover. It is of considerable value because of
his well informed account of close air support activity
during the first few months of the war.

290 Docker, Charles L. "Marine Air Over Korea" Marine
Corps Gazette 69:12 (December 1985) 38-50, photos.
     Discusses the extent of the Marine Corps operations
over Korea in support of ground troops. The Marines and
Air Force covered this war differently.

291 Dolan, Michael J. "Mosquito and Horsefly" Combat
Forces Journal 2:7 (February 1952) 35-37.
     Army spotter planes (L5) worked so well in
directing ground support that the Air Force sent out
mosquito planes to replace them performing air
observation duties.

292 Futrell, Robert F. and Albert F. Simpson. "Air War in Korea" <u>Air University Quarterly Review</u> 4:2 (Fall, 1950) 18-39; 4:3 (Spring, 1951) 47-67; 4:4 (September, 1951) 83-89.
        Concerned initial reaction to the invasion, use of air to support ground troops, and strategic bombing.

293 Gray, Robert L. "Air Operations Over Korea" <u>Army Information Digest</u> 7 (1951) 16-23.
        Concerns the first year of operations against North Korea and points out that much of their ability to provide group support was the result of the lack of any significant aerial opposition. This made it possible to provide close support for ground troops almost at will, and to attack long range supply routes.

294 Grogan, Stanley Jr. "Lightening Lancers: Combat Highlights of the 68th Squadron in Korea" <u>Airplane History</u> 9 (1962) 249-252.
        From their role as escort cover for the first flights of evacuees to the first use of night fighters the 68th Squadron was early and heavily involved in the Korean War.

295 Harrity, Ralph D. "A Forward Observer Reports from Korea" <u>Combat Forces Journal</u> 1:9 (April 1951) 28-29.
        The role of the forward observer, never very safe, increased in importance during the fluid nature of the first weeks of fighting. In most cases any observation for direct fire came from the observer, who was also the only eyes available to many small unit commanders.

296 Key, William G. "Air Power in Action: Korea, 1950-51" <u>Pegasus</u> 17 (1951) 1-16.
        Looks at the effect of United States air operations during the first full year of the war.

297 Knight, Charlotte. "Air War in Korea" <u>Air Force</u> 33 (1950) 21-25.
        A war correspondent examines the United States air operations during the first few months of the war. She traces their efforts to halt the North Korean advance across the 38th and heading south.

298   Knight, Charlotte. "Korea: A Twenty-Fifth Anniversary" <u>Air Force</u> 58 (1975) 59-63.

Based on an August 1950 field report during which the author tries to describe and evaluate the air operations during the first few months of war. The article is supportive of the American air effort but not of the effect.

299   Kropf, Roger F. "The US Air Force in Korea: Problems that Hindered the Effectiveness of Air Power" <u>Airpower Journal</u> 4:1 (Spring 1990) 30-46.

A rather ambitious attempt to deal with the problems which seemed to hinder a greater success for the Air Force in the Korean War. The author identifies the problems as poorly selected air bases, difficulty of the joint command structure, and poor air-to-ground coordination.

300 Launius, Roger A. "MATS and the Korean War Airlift" <u>Airlift</u> 12:2 (Summer 1990) 16-21.

Brief history by this NASA historian concerning the Military Air Transport System during the early phase and the prolonged need to move men and equipment in and out of Korea.

301   Martin, Harold H. "How Our Air Raiders Plastered Korea" <u>Saturday Evening Post</u> 223 (1950) 26-27, 88-90.

Considers the different Far East Commands operating in the early war period, 25 June to 4 July 1950. Deals with the various roles of air and naval flight operations in Korea during this week and a half of the early fighting.

302 Park, Sun E. "Operation Dragonfly" <u>US Army Aviation Digest</u> 27 (1981) 7-9.

The aviation section of the United States 24th Infantry provided the first use of air reconnaissance for ground troop in July of 1950. The effort was so successful it became the model for the creation of an operational unit, known as the Mosquitos, in August of 1950.

303   Ragle, George L. "Dragonflies Over Korea" Combat
Forces Journal 1:4 (November 1950) 32-33.
    The small observer planes used by the army (L4 in
this case) played a series of very significant roles in
addition to their assigned observation duties. During
the   early   days   of   fighting   the   24th   Infantry
particularly, used them for carrying ammo, wounded, fire
direction, supplies to cut off units, and for various
commander's direct observation of troop displacement.

304   Sleeper, Raymond S. "Korean Targets for Medium
Bombardment" Air University Quarterly Review 4:3 (Spring
1951) 21.
    Story of the early air attacks by B-29s, the
difficulty of finding targets for the massive bombers,
and the use of the heavy bombs during the early battles
in July and August of 1950.

305 Spaatz, Carl. "Why We Face a Tough Fight in Korea"
Newsweek 36 (July 10, 1950) 23.
    Decries the failure of ground forces to take
advantage of the major bombing runs. The lack of
adequate ground response means that the North Koreans
could save most of their supplies, and move quickly.
The advantage of American airpower is diminished if
North Korean troops are able to save their supplies.

306   Sugar, Jim. "Korea: 35 Years After MIG Alley"
Flying 113 (December 1986) 60-68.
    A recounting of the Air Force first response to the
North   Korean   invasion,   and   the   difficulties   of
reactivation.

307 "United States Air Force Operation in the Korean
Conflict, 25 June - 1 November 1950"   Operational
Research Office United States Air Force Historical
Study, No. 71 (July 1952) 44.
    A restricted monograph written to show the extent
and success of the Air Force. It was expanded and
published in book form by Robert Futrell.

308   United States Secretary of Defense "Air War in Korea" Air University Quarterly Review 4 (1950) 19-39.
An official assessment of United States Air Force operations in Korea, 25 June to 1 November 1950. The not too surprising conclusion is that the Air Force did well. Despite the somewhat self-serving attitude this is an excellent source for statistics on sorties flown, targets, when delivered, and how they related to the ground war.

309   Wallrich, William. "Bedcheck Charlie Flies Again" Air Force (September 1953) 110-113.
Every war seems to create its "bedcheck" incidents. In this case the trials of troops dealing with a light flying North Korean plane that came to harass the troops at night. Talks about the difficulties of catching or destroying the slow moving plane.

310   Weyland, O. P. "The Air Campaign in Korea" Air University Quarterly Review 6:3 (Fall 1953) 3-28.
This brief account presents an overly optimistic view of the success of both air-to-ground support and strategic bombing.

Marines as Separate Units

BOOKS

311   Geer, Andrew. The New Breed, The Story of the U. S. Marines in Korea. New York: Harper and Brothers, 1952. 395 pages, index, maps.
This is the story of the United States Marines in Korea. While the Marines came reasonably late to the battle, early August 1950, their presence made a considerable difference both in terms of morale and in terms of available fighting men. The 5th Marine Brigade was pushed into battle almost immediately upon arrival, and held their section of the Pusan Perimeter during some of the heaviest fighting. See pages 7-12, 40, 86-99 and as indexed.

312   Hammel, Eric M.   Chosin: Heroic Ordeal of the
Korean War. New York: Vanguard Press, 1981. 457 pages,
index, maps.

More a history of the development of marine forces
in Korea it concentrates on the post-Pusan period.
However the early chapters provide background, and
throughout there is steady reference to events at Pusan
and during the breakout. Well indexed, but especially
79-84.

313   Mobilization of the Marine Corps Reserve in the
Korean Conflict 1950-1951. Washington, DC: History
Branch G-3 Division, United States Marine Corps, 1967.
77 page typescript at Command and Staff College,
Leavenworth, Kansas.

A short history recalling the identification and
call-up of marine units and individuals, plus the
movement of marine troops to fill existing combat
groups, and shipment.

314 Montross, Lynn.   Cavalry of the Sky: The Story of
U. S. Marine Combat Helicopters. New York: Harper &
Brothers,   Publisher,   1954.   270   pages,   index,
photographs, maps, charts, bibliography.

A brief history of the development of helicopter
combat units, the training, and their deployment and use
in Korea. Montross does his usual in-depth research and
is an excellent source of the use of helicopters for
both combat and rescue. When MacArthur asked for the
marines, he included in his request the first active
helicopter unit. See chapter seven.

315   Montross, Lynn and Nicholas A. Canzona. U. S.
Marine Operations in Korea, 1950-1953. Volume 1. The
Pusan Perimeter. Washington, DC: Historical Branch,
Headquarters, G-3, U. S. Marine Corps, 1954. Maps.

A detailed account of the United States Marine
contribution to the Korean War from their first
encounter with communist troops, until the second battle
of Naktong River. Operations of the 1st Provisional
Brigade and Marine Air Group 33 from their landing 2
August 1950 until their withdrawal on 13 September 1950.

ARTICLES

316   Canzona, Nicholas A. "A Hill Near Yongsan" <u>Marine Corps Gazette</u> 39 (1955) 55-59.
    Accounts of the 1st and 2nd Battalion, 5th Marines during the bloody Second Naktong River campaign in September of 1950.

317 Canzona, Nicholas A. "Marines Land at Pusan, Korea, August 1950" <u>Marine Corps Gazette</u> 69 (August 1985) 42-46+, illustrations.
    An interview with this famous military historian about the first landings and early fighting of the marines who were first deployed at the Pusan Perimeter in Korea.

318   Chung, Ul Mun. "Letter From Almond"   <u>Leatherneck</u> 36:4 (1953) 34-35.
    A Korean interpreter comments on his early months with the 7th Marines.

319 Conner, John. "The New Breed" <u>Collier's</u> 126 (1950) 71-72.
    Accounts for the 1st Marine Brigade during the first two months of the Korean War, including time along the defensive lines of the Pusan Perimeter, and prior to the pull-out for the Inchon landing.

320 Fenton, Francis I. "Changallon Valley" <u>Marine Corps Gazette</u> 35 (1951) 48-53.
    Describes the activities of the men of Company B. 1st Marine Battalion, 5th Marines who fought a fierce battle during the ambush at Sachon on the 12th of August 1950.

321   Martin, Harold H. "The Epic of Bloody Hill" <u>Saturday Evening Post</u> 223 (1950) 50-54, 59-60.
    Describes the bitter fighting at Bloody Hill where the men of the 1st Provisional Marine Brigade made a significant stand near the crossing of the Naktong River.

322 Martin, Harold H.   "The Ordeal of Marine Squad 2"
Saturday Evening Post 223 (1950) 24-25, 126-130, 133.
     Martin follows the action of a marine rifle squad
from mid July when they arrived until 17 August 1950.
Involved in heavy fighting the squad lost four who died
and five who where seriously wounded.

323 Montross, Lynn.   "The Pusan Perimeter: Fight For
a Foothold" Marine Corps Gazette 35 (June 1951) 30-39.
Illustrations, maps.
     Montross,   in   making   the   case   for   the   1st
Provisional Marine Brigade serving from 7 August to 7
September 1950, tends to forget the harsh and desperate
fighting of United States, Republic of Korea, and some
United Nations troops which held the line for months.
Follows operations of 1st Provisional Marines from 7
August to 7 September 1950 which helped to establish and
hold the United Nations defense command at the Pusan
Perimeter.   The second in a series of Gazette articles
which are designed to provide an official look at marine
action in Korea.   The first "Mobilization and Movement
to Korea" and the second dealing with the marines who
arrived on 2 August 1950 and fought at the Perimeter.

324 Murray, R. L. "The First Naktong" Marine Corps
Gazette 49 (November 1965) 84-85.
     Brief account of the fighting between the North
Koreans and the marines along the Naktong River during
the bloody days from 17-19 August 1950. Reminds the
reader that the marines were fighting along the Naktong
River in the early 1950s.

325 Parry, Francis F. "Marine Artillery in Korea: Part
I, Ready or Not" Marine Corps Gazette 71:6 (June 1987)
47-52.
     Brief memoirs of a man who was a battalion
commander of a marine artillery outfit. Researchers
often forget that the marines provided much of their own
artillery support.

326   Tallent, Robert W. "Pusan -- A Stop Enroute" _Leatherneck_ 33 (1950) 14-17.
        Traces the pull-out of the 1st Provisional Marines who in the midst of a desperate fight to save Pusan, were pulled out to prepare for the Inchon landing. At a time when the success of the defense was in serious question, and against Walker's requests, MacArthur pulled the marines out, for rest and regrouping, prior to the invasion.

327   Tapplet, R. D. and R. E. Whipple. "Darkhorse Sets the Pace" _Marine Corps Gazette_ 37:6:7 (June-July 1950) 14-23, 44-50. Maps, views.
        Combat activities of the Third Battalion, Fifth Marines in Korea, 1950.

Logistics, Support, and Leadership

BOOKS

328 Dunstan, Simon. _Armour of the Korean War 1950-1953_. London: Osprey   Publishing,   1982.   41   pages, illustrations.
        Brief illustrated history of the heavy armor used by both the United States and the North Korean during the war.   The static nature of the war limited tanks later in the fighting but it was such armor that moved the North Koreans rapidly south.   Illustrations are excellent.

329   Gough, Terrence J. _U. S. Army Mobilization and Logistics in the Korean War_. Washington, DC: Center of Military History, 1987. 125 pages.
        Discusses the difficulty of initial mobilization and logistical support during the early and middle period of the Korean War. Considers military commanders and their lack of respect for logistical problems.

330 Huston, James A. Guns and Butter, Powder and Rice:
U. S. Army Logistics in the Korean War. Selinsgrove:
Susquehanna University Press, 1989. 492 pages, index,
bibliography, illustrations. See chapters one - four.
     The abrupt nature of the Korean invasion, and
America's response made it particularly hard on those
responsible for supply. The first hundred pages of this
work explains how it was possible to deliver a troop
build-up of nearly 100,000 men and to provide 2 million
tons of supplies prior to the Pusan breakout. The
answer was fairly simply. For the first three months of
the war in Korea it was fought with World War II
supplies, a good portion of it considered obsolete at
the time of its use. 100-113.

331   James, D. Clayton with Anne Sharp Wells.
Refighting the Last War: Command and Crisis in Korea,
1950-1953. New York: Free Press, 1992. 400 pages,
index, photographs.
     A reinterpretation of the high command in Korea, it
examines six major decisions, and reviews the roles,
leadership ability, personalities and prejudices of the
top five commanders. Argues all were limited by
perceptions learned in World War II.

332 Kahn, Ely J. The Peculiar War: Impressions of a
Reporter in Korea. New York: Random House, 1952. 211
pages.
     Considers the Korean War, but gives a lot of
attention to the early military leaders, their
prejudices and failures, as well as the successes
enjoyed.

333 Kaufman, Burton I. The Korean War: Challenges in
Crisis, Credibility, and Command. Philadelphia: Temple
University Press, 1986. 381 pages, index, map.
     Concerned with command failures early in the war.
Chapters one and two deal with the conspiracy of
intervention and command, with the significance of the
Pusan Perimeter which stabilized the war and allowed for
an eventual American withdrawal with honor. It asks the
generally unanswered question as to whether the Inchon
landing was necessary or did it simply escalate the war.

334   Stanton, Shelby. US Army Uniforms of the Korean War. Pennsylvania: Stackpole, 1992. 243 pages, index.
Account of uniforms available during early months, the difficulty of supply, and the inappropriateness of what was available. Supply problem considered page 1-17.

335 Thompson, Annis G. The Great Airlift: The Story of Combat Cargo. Tokyo: Dai-Nippon Printing Company, 1954. 463 pages, 50% pictures.
Primarily a report of the role of the 315th Air Division in supplying the troops early in the war.

336   Westover, John G.   Combat Support in Korea. Washington, DC: Center of Military History, Government Printing Office, 1987.
This edition of the U. S. Army in Action Series, is an excellent account of the logistical problems created by the conflict in Korea, and how the American Army was able to address them. This is primarily an oral history report provided by men on the spot dealing with the logistical concerns from the opening days of the war.

ARTICLES

337   Arrington, Leonard J. et al "Sentinels on the Desert: The Dunway Proving Grounds (1942-1963) and the Desert Chemical Depot (1942-1955)" Utah Historical Review 32:1 (1964) 32-43.
A short history of the Dunway Center for chemical warfare research shows how the outbreak of war in Korea led to reactivation and expansion of the facilities. Became a problem when charges of chemical warfare were leveled against the Americans.

338   Arrington, Leonard J. and Thomas G. Alexander. "Supply Hub of the West: Defense Depot Ogden" Utah Historical Quarterly 32:2 (1964) 99-121.
An account of the impact of the Korean War on the Defense Depot at Ogden, Utah, where in 1950 125,093 tons of material was shipped to the front. Describes the expansion of facilities, and the shipping of World War II remains.

339 Boyd, Ralph C. and John G. Westover. "Truck Platoon
-- Withdrawal from Taejon" Combat Forces Journal 3:2
(September 1952) 26-27.
     Deals with the difficulty of supply and transport
during the early days of the war.   During July and
August of 1950, trucks running out of Pusan harbor were
used to move retreating men and equipment and to deliver
much needed supplies.

340 "Call to Arms Against World Aggression" Newsweek
36 (July 31, 1950) 22.
     Twenty-five days after the communist's aggression,
the President calls for ten billion dollars, the
National Guard, and more military assistance to NATO.

341 Flanagan, William J. "Korean War Logistics: The
First Hundred Days" Army Logistics 18 (March - April,
1986) 34-38.
     Takes a brief look at the problems with supply and
distribution during the first three months of the war.
Not only were there limited supplies in Japan, there
were few supplies anywhere. What army logistics was
able to accomplish was not far short of a miracle.

342 Flynn, George Q. "The Draft and College Deferments
During the Korean War" Historian 50 (May 1988) 369-385.
     When the Korean War broke out the army was
depleted. Peace efforts and reorganization had limited
the size of the military and when it became evident that
troops were going to be needed the draft went into
action. Though the push was on and the need was great,
the system was poorly manned and many a young man
avoided the draft with a series of deferments.

343 Fowle, Barry C.   "Civil Works and Military
Construction" Engineers 5 (January 1991) 48-49.
     The story of the 14th Engineer Combat Battalion
(ECB) of the 1st Cavalry Division who arrived in Korea
in July of 1950. The battalion served as infantry
during much of this time, but also worked on the
destruction of key bridges across the Naktong River. A
short but excellent piece about combat engineers at
Pusan.

344   Garn, Phil R. "75 mm Recoilless Rifle in Korea"
Combat Forces Journal 2:9 (April 1952) 23-25.
     The 75 mm recoilless rifle was first introduced in
Korea in August 1950 and was used at Tongmyongwon where
it was proved to be very effective. The 75 mm was one
of the most powerful infantry-support weapons available,
and gave the troops a new attitude toward North Korean
tanks. The difficulty of the mountainous terrain in
Korea made it necessary to provide a large number of
support troops for this crew served weapon.

345 "Logistics: By Sea and Air to Korea" Combat Forces
Journal 1:3 (October 1950) 46.
     In part this article is a comment on a story that
appeared in Life (September 1950) which seemed to
express amazement at the amount of supplies reaching
Pusan. The combined journal provided some statistics on
the amount of supplies being provided and to confirm
both the large amounts and the excellent way they are
delivered. The response to logistic needs, and the
amazing build-up during the Pusan Perimeter period, is
one of the success stories of the war.

346 Owens, Richard W. "AA Makes the Team" Combat Forces
Journal 3:10 (May 1953) 27-29.
     It was an AA outfit (quad fifties) which drew the
first enemy blood as they downed a plane on the fourth
day of battle. These quad fifties were put on the bed
of the workhorse "Duce-and-a-Half" trucks and easily
moved. While also available as antiaircraft many AA
units were assigned as self-propelled support units with
the infantry. In this role they proved to be very
effective against massed troops.

347 "What's the Use of Korea?" Life 31 (August 6, 1951)
28.
     One of the key elements in General MacArthur's
eventual replacement was a series of "unwise," and
generally unnecessary, speeches given. This is the
report of one such speech given by MacArthur, in which
he suggests the "utter uselessness of the Korean War."
Regardless of what he meant, the power of the suggestion
was harmful to the troops.

Medical Support

BOOKS

348   Cowdery, Albert E.   United States Army in the Korean War: Medic's War. Washington, DC: Chief of Military History, 1987. 409 pages, photographs.
    Pusan harbor was not only the center of logistical support, it was the only available evacuation point for the wounded which came in increasing numbers. As the Perimeter developed, the army set up both an evacuation system and an immediate response hospital as early as mid-July.   This official history of the medical department discusses the retreat, the defense, and the breakout from the medical point of view. Of particular interest was the growing use of the helicopter as a medical evacuation vehicle. Indexed, but especially 79-97.

349   White, William L.   Back Down the Ridge.   New York: Harcourt Brace, 1953. 182 pages.
    An account of a mobile army surgical hospital; "the story of some typical Korean casualties: how they came by their wounds, how they were gotten down off the ridge to a battalion aid station, and what happened then."

ARTICLES

350   Bower, Warner F. "Evacuating Wounded from Korea" Army Information Digest 5:12 (December 1950) 47-54.
    Discusses   the   speed   with   which   the   medical community overcame the difficulty of casualty care, and established the line from the "front to California."

351   "Casualties: The Toll Rises"   Newsweek   37 (February 5, 1951) 26.
    Reports that United States casualties had now exceeded the number of men in seven full American divisions. 15,000 men being sent to Korea monthly.

352 Ewin, JV Haasem. "Fighting For Life in Korea" <u>Asian Defense Journal</u> (December 1989) 92-96.
    The medical resources and the care for wounded in the early days of the Korean War have much to teach us about the nature of our United Nations preparedness. The high costs that were paid for not being well prepared cannot be repaid.

353 Hume, Edgar E. "United Nations Medical Service in the Korean Conflict" <u>Military Surgeon</u> 109 (1951) 91-95.
    A look at the United Nations activities, including the multi-national force provisions for medical service. The need, and initial response, felt during the first few months of the war is reviewed.

354 Marsh, Walter. "Army Surgical Hospitals at Work in Korea" <u>Army Information Digest</u> 8 (1953) 48-52.
    Describes the utilization of Army Surgical Hospitals during the first months of the war when three such units were in operation. Located behind the lines they performed most major surgery required. Medical evacuation was cut considerably by the success of these units.

355 Morgan, Len. "M*A*S*H Epilogue" <u>Flying</u> 110 (March 1983) 60-63.
    Using the popular TV series as background, the author discusses the early role of the Mobile Medical units, the introduction of the helicopter ambulances, and their success particularly during the early days of the war.

356 Thornton, W. H. "The 24th Division Medical Battalion in Korea" <u>Military Surgeon</u> 113 (1953) 27-31.
    Traces the 24th Division Medical battalion (as an example) during the first two months of the war. Takes into accounts the difficulty of the abrupt move from Japan, setting up a medical service with such limited supplies, and providing medical aid during the long retreat.

Correspondents and the Perimeter

BOOK

357   Moeller, Susan D.   Shooting War: Photography and
the American Combat Experience. New York: Basic Books,
1991. 474 pages, index, photographs.
    Part four "The Korean War" (251-324) deals with the
role of, and use of, combat photography during the
Korean Conflict. Asserts photojournalist were less
restricted than other correspondents.

ARTICLES

358   "Are You Telling Them That It is an Utterly Useless
War?" History 18:1 (Winter 1976) 110-111.
    A discussion of Phillip Knightley's The First
Casualty in which the role of the war correspondent,
especially early in this war, is compared to the
reporting of other wars. Knightley's work seems to feel
that the troops were not being told the truth, either as
to what they were doing, or how well they were doing it.

359   Cleary, Thomas J. Jr. "Aid and Comfort to the
Enemy" Military Review 48 (August 1968) 51-55.
    During the first few weeks of the fighting, the
United States press corps managed to print every bit of
military information they got their hands one, including
a great deal about the limitations of troops and
supplies, which aided the enemy in fighting the war.
Local and jurisdictional commanders quickly put a lid on
the press but a lot of information still got out.

360 Dorn, Frank. "Briefing the Press" Army Information
Digest 6 (1951) 36-41.
    Describes the procedure by which the Department of
Defense disseminated news to the press during the first
six months. The news that was released rarely told the
American people what was happening, and was especially
quiet about the difficulties involved.

361 Erwin, Ray. "Censorship, Communications Worry 200 K-War Correspondence" Education Public 83 (1950) 7, 44.

Discusses the problems of war correspondents during the early weeks of the war. Rules of reporting constantly changed. The confusion was not simply policy. This article's value is that it includes the names of most correspondents on the scene at the time.

Analysis

BOOKS

362 Carew, Tim. Korea: The Commonwealth at War. London: Cassell, 1967. 307 pages, index, photographs, maps, appendix.

The author lists his work as an expose of military ineptitude. He makes an excellent case for such failure during the first few weeks, stressing American concern that the United Nations was so slow to send troops. His account of British troops, joining in the battle of August 1950, during the fighting south west of Taegu is very informative. Chapters one to four discuss America as the major force, and supplier.

363 Heller, Francis H. (editor). The Korean War: A 25-Year Perspective. Lawrence: Regents Press, 1977. 251 pages.

A series of essays concerning the Korean War, and showing a good deal of hind sight. Chapter four which deals with the Korean War and the response of the American society, and chapter two, the report on a panel of officers, are the most helpful. General Collins explains why it was that General Walker's retreat and defense of Pusan has been so poorly understood, and yet was so vital.

364 Herbert, Anthony B. with James T. Wooten. Soldier. New York: Holt, 1973. 498 pages, illustrations.

Autobiography of Master Sergeant (later Lt. Colonel) Anthony Herbert who was identified as the nation's "outstanding soldier" of the Korean War and was court-marshalled and relieved as a Regimental Commander during the Vietnam War.

365   MacDonald, Callum A.   Korea: The War Before
Vietnam. New York: The Free Press, 1986. 330 pages,
index, photographs.

   A particularly fine book deals with the geo-
politics of the war, seeing the implications for the
cold war as well as for the relationships between
allies.   Does not believe that either American or
Russian foreign policy would be able to stand up well
under scrutiny. Does not deal with Pusan other than as
one of the many questions to be considered, primarily by
MacArthur, in the attempt to formulate a war policy.

366 Marshall, Samuel L. A. and Cate Marshall. (editor).
Bringing Up the Rear: A Memoir. San Francisco: Presidio
Press, 1979. 310 pages, index, photographs, maps.

   Marshall, one of America's most respected military
historians, saw military service for over thirty years
and wrote his history of his role in military affairs.
Includes opinion and analysis of the defense at Pusan.

367 Rees, David. (editor). The Korean War: History and
Tactics. New York: Crescent, 1984. 128 pages, index,
photographs.

   Good single volume of the military aspects of the
war. Best treatment of policy in relation to military
operations. Highly supportive and considers "American
involvement in Korea, the greatest act in recent
American history."

                    ARTICLES

368 Cottrell, Alvin J. and James E. Dougherty. "The
Lessons of Korea: War and the Power of Man" Orbis 39-64.

   An interesting account of the impact of limited
war, and the failure of the United States to see the
Korean Conflict in light of its strategic background.

369 DeWeerd, Harvey A.   "Lessons of the Korean War"
Yale Review 40 (Summer 1951) 592-603.

   At the time of its writing, the author saw the
Korean war as undeclared, limited, of minor importance,
in general a confusing event which has already taught
some important lessons. These lessons seem to be valid
though he wrote before the war was over.

370   Hamby, Alonzo L.   "Public Opinion: Korea and Vietnam" Wilson Quarterly 2 (Summer 1978).
    Asserts a comparison between the American attitude toward Korea and Vietnam, finding that the protests against the Korean War came from the political Right, who used and honored the American flag in their protests.

371 Kriebel, P. Wesley. "Unfinished Business -- Intervention Under the U. N. Umbrella: America's Participation in the Korean War, 1950-1953"   Robin D. Higham. (editor).   Intervention or Abstention: The Dilemma of American Foreign Policy.   Lexington: University Press of Kentucky, 1975.   221 pages, bibliography. 114-128.
    In this article the author attempts to identify the attitude of the communist states about American policy, and the ultimate decision to intervene in the Korean War.

372   Lindley, Ernest.   "Counters to the Kremlin's Designs" Newsweek   36 (July 31, 1950) 20-21.
    This author maintains that if the Korean attack was intended as a diversionary action preluding to a Russian attack on Western Europe, it was not well done. And the prompt action by the United States prevented the Russians from being successful.

373 Morton, Louis. "Twin Essentials of a Limited War" Army 11:6 (January 1961) 47.
    Limited war is essential to our freedom and can only be fought when those involved accept two things: the freedom to negotiate and a self-imposed restriction on the use of weapons.

374 Stilwell, Richard. "A Victory Not to Be Forgotten" The American Legion (June 1990) 30, 49-50.
    Stilwell holds that the Korean war was pivotal in postwar history and politics and thus beneficial to the United States and Allies.   Appears to be overly patriotic.

Other Sources

Dissertations and Theses

375   Burk, Richard J. "The Organization and Command of United Nations Military Forces" Master's thesis, Yale University, New Haven, 1956.

Traces the difficulties encountered by attempts at a United Nations Command. The early days were fairly simple with only American and ROK troops involved, but during the Pusan Perimeter the landing of other troops and the involvement of other nationalities in the naval units, brought the difficulties to a head.

376   Hakon, Ostholm. "The First Year of the Korean War: The Road Toward Armistice" Ph.D. dissertation, Kent State University, 1982. 267 pages.

Holds that the Korean War was the most catastrophic of the international conflicts. The event created a situation no one wanted. Chapter four deals with the effect of this view on the fighting of the war, and discusses the dangers seen by the military leadership involved in the war.

377   Johnson, Lisa D. "No Place for a Woman: A Biographical Study of War Correspondent Marguerite Higgins." Master's thesis, East Texas State University, 1983.

Marguerite Higgins would have disagreed with the author for she felt it was very much her place to be there. This thesis describes Higgins as a very aggressive correspondent during the early phases of the war, where she sent daily dispatches despite the misgivings of the military commanders.

378   Mantell, Matthew E. "Opposition to the Korean War: A Study in American Dissent" Ph.D. dissertation, New York, 1973.

Considers American opposition to the Korean War and finds it comes from the pacifist movement, the political left who considered the war imperialistic, and the pragmatists who originally supported the war but soon felt it was not a war that could be won.

379   Stelmach, Daniel S.   "The Influence of Russian Armored Tactics on the North Korean Invasion, 1950" Ph.D. dissertation, Washington University, St. Louis. 1973.
    A detailed analysis of the impressive showing of Russian tanks, manned by North Korean tankers, and using Russian tactics, during the early days of the invasion. Stresses the ruthless efficiency of the Soviet military advisors. Describes the Russian role in equipping and training the North Korean Army. The author provides an in-depth look at the experience of North Korean tankers in July and August of 1950, as well as the triangular base of armor-infantry-artillery used so effectively.

Pictorial Histories

BOOKS

380 Cassino, Jay A. (editor). Pictorial History of the Korean War. New York: Wise, 1951.
    Covers the early United Nations forces during the beginning stages of the conflict. This edition was identified as the memorial edition for the Veterans of Foreign Wars.

381 Duncan, David. This is War! A Photo-Narrative of the Korean War. New York: Little, 1990.
    Duncan, a world class photo-journalist covers the United States Marines fighting in Korea. A short text and uncaptioned photography tells a graphic story. While it covers the whole war there is plenty of coverage of the defense of Pusan Perimeter.

382 Giangreco, Dennis M. War in Korea, 1950-1953. Novato, California: Presidio Press, 1990. 331 pages.
    Pictorial history of the Korean War with several new photographs, many very descriptive, as well as an excellent set of captions. Pages 1-66 deal with the pre-Inchon period.

383 Veterans of Foreign Wars. <u>Pictorial History of the Korean War</u>. np: Veterans Historical Book Service, 1954.
     In this very complete collection, the various photographs are used to explain the numerous aspects of the United Nations Command.

Films

BOOK

384 Butler, Lucius A. and Chaesoon T. Youngs. <u>Films for Korean Studies</u>. Honolulu: Center for Korean Studies, 1978.
     Identifies more than one hundred and twenty 16mm films on different aspects of the Korean War. Lists some films on the early phases of the war including Pusan Perimeter.

ARTICLES

385 Altieri, James J. "The Story Behind Army Feature Films" <u>Army Information Digest</u> 7 (1952) 37-42.
     Army cooperation on the production of Korean War films, of which more than 35 feature films were finally made. Uses "The Big Push" as an illustration.

386 Hulse, Ed. "The Forgotten War" <u>Video Review</u> (November 1990) 57.
     A review of Korean War movies. What is surprising is how few of them were of any merit, or had any popularity.

FILMS

387 <u>Korea: The Forgotten War</u>. Produced by Media Home Entertainment, Video.
     A really excellent film which shows the war at its most confusing state.

388 <u>Korea: The Forgotten War</u>. Library Video Company, sound, black and white. Distributed Library Video.

389   Korea: The Forgotten War.   Video, 92 min, color,
b&w. Los Angeles, California: Fox Hills Video, 1987.
     Fairly common account, using actual footage without
much commentary.   More interested with the Chinese
period of the war, but some early accounting.

390 The Korean War. Video, 30 min, b&w, color, GM-2585,
Princeton, New Jersey: Films for the Humanities and
Sciences.
     Covers the partitioning of Korea; the battles for
Seoul, Pusan, General MacArthur's famous speeches, all
a part of this film presenting one last remaining moment
of the East-West confrontation.

391   Motion Picture History of the Korean War.   Video,
59 min, b&w. Marina Del Ray, California: Aviation
Heritage Series.   NFV, 1988.
     Covers all phases of the fighting from the outbreak
of hostilities, on 25 June 1950, to the signing of the
armistice on 27 July 1953.

392   Korea: MacArthur's War. MP1518, 60 min, sound,
black and white. Distributed MPI Home Video.
     Another view of MacArthur and Korea.

393   Korea, MacArthur's War. Video, 54 min, b&w. MPI
Home Video, 1988.
     Examines the highly charged Korean War and
critically analyzes the reasons for it, as well as
MacArthur's role in it.

394   Korea: The Unknown War.   Produced by Austin Hoyt
and Phillip Whitehead.
     An attempt at a general coverage but is not well
done. A six part PBS TV program.

395   Meeting the Red Challenge.   Series. b&w, 16mm, 14
min, 1959. D-4.
     The events leading up to the Korean War, the
Communist invasion of South Korea, and the role of
United States air power is pictured.

396   A Motion Picture History of the Korean War.
Washington, DC: Department of Defense, 1981. 58 min,
sound, b&w. Distributed by National Audio-Visual Center.

397   Truman and the Korean War. The Truman Years.   18
min, b&w, TVT. D-3.
    Truman convened the Security Council of the United
Nations to vote for intervention.

398   The Twenty-Fourth Infantry Division. Color, 16mm,
28 min. D-1. CMF 130-7722 (SAVPIN 30279).
    The division's reactivation during the Korean
conflict is considered.

399   USA Wars: Korea. Quanta Press, Inc., 1991.
    A disc which provides 1071 photographs, oral
interviews, and narratives concerning the war.

400   War in the 'Land That God Forgot': Korea 1950-1953.
Feature Film.
    Never located.

Fiction

BOOK

401   Ross, Glen. The Last Campaign. New York: Harper,
1962.
    Fictional account of a young army corporal who was
stationed in Japan in 1950 in the division band. When
the war broke out he and his friends were sent off to
Korea in that first group whose primary role was to make
an appearance. The idea was still held that just having
Americans there would stem the tide. Describes the
horrors and suffering they experienced.

APPENDIX

Major United States Ground Forces in Korea, 1950

Eighth Army

I Corps

IX Corps

X Corps

1st Cavalry Division
     Units of this division date back to 1855 under the
command of Robert E. Lee. "First in Name and Battle"
they were the first Americans into liberated Manila and
the first military unit in Tokyo.

2d Infantry Division
     "Second to None", the Indian Head Division was
activated in Texas, and during World War One received
more decorations than any other American division.
Landing on Omaha Beach on D+1 they fought through the
Battle of the Bulge to Czechoslovakia

3d Infantry Division

7th Infantry Division
    The inverted and upright "7" provided the Hour Glass Division its patch.   Activated in 1940 under Joseph Stilwell in California it recaptured the first American soil at Attu, fought at Kwajalein, Eniwetok, Leyte, and Okinawa.

11th Airborne Division (187th RCT)

24th Infantry Division
    Formed from the old Hawaiian Division in 1941 (source of their Taro leaf patch) they suffered at Pearl Harbor, New Guinea, Leyte, and were the first troops into Korea.

25th Infantry Division
    Tropic Lightning Division, formed from the Old Hawaiian Division (Taro leaf with lightning strike patch) fought its way from Guadalcanal and New Georgia to Luzon.   At the time it included the famed   24th Infantry Regiment.

1st Marine Division
    Created from the First Brigade, known as the "Raggedy Ann Marines" in 1941. Immortalized the victory at Guadalcanal with the Southern Cross on its patch, fought at Cape Gloucester, Peleliu and Okinawa.

United Nations Forces in Korea in September, 1950

Ground Forces:

Australia	Infantry Battalion
Belgium	Infantry Battalion
Canada	Brigade Group
France	Infantry Battalion
Greece	Unit Land Forces
Netherlands	Infantry Battalion
New Zealand	One combat unit
Philippines	Regimental Combat Team

Thailand	Infantry Combat Team
Turkey	Infantry Combat Force
United Kingdom	Two Brigades
United States	1st Cavalry Division
	2nd Infantry Division
	24th Infantry Division
	25th Infantry Division
	First Marine Division

Naval Forces:

Australia	Two Destroyers
	One Aircraft Carrier
	One Frigate
Canada	Three Destroyers
France	One Patrol Gun Boat
Netherlands	One Destroyer
New Zealand	Two Frigates
United Kingdom	Naval Forces in Japan
	One Aircraft Carrier
	Two Cruisers
	Eight Destroyers
	One Survey Ship
United States	Fast Carrier Task
	Group, with escort

Air Forces:

Australia	One RAAR Fighter Squadron
	Base Unit w/communication
Canada	One RCAF Squadron
Union of South Africa	One Fighter Squadron
	Base ground personnel
United Kingdom	Elements of the Air Force
United States	One Tactical Air Force,
	Bombardment Command
	Combat Air Command

Transport and Materials:

Canada	Facilities of Canadian Pacific Airlines to Tokyo
	Dry Cargo Vessel
Greece	Eight Dakota transport planes
Norway	Merchant Ship
Panama	Use of Merchant Marine Corps for transport
Philippines	17 Sherman Tanks
	1 tank destroyer
United Kingdom	Seven Supply Vehicles
United States	Air Transport Supply Vehicles

Medical Services:

Denmark	Hospital Ship
India	Field Ambulance Unit
Sweden	Field Hospital Unit
United Kingdom	Hospital Ship
United States	Large scale hospital facilities

INDEX OF
PERIODICALS REVIEWED

AUTHOR INDEX

Unless noted, numbers refer to entries.

SUBJECT INDEX

Unless noted, numbers refer to entries.

About the Compiler

PAUL M. EDWARDS, Dean of the Graduate College of Park College in Kansas City, Missouri, is a specialist in Korean, military, and bibliographical history who has written at length on these subjects. He is the founder of the Center for Study of the Korean Conflict, a library and archival foundation in Independence, Missouri. He served with the 31st Field Artillery in Korea and has his Ph.D. in transatlantic history from the University of St. Andrews in Scotland. His most recent book is *General Matthew B. Ridgway: An Annotated Bibliography* (Greenwood Press, 1993).